HOW TO BUILD BUZZ FOR YOUR BIZ

TAP INTO THE POWER OF SOCIAL MEDIA, PUBLICITY, AND RELATIONSHIP MARKETING TO GROW YOUR BUSINESS

Wendy Nelson Kenney

Published by 23 Kazoos, LLC

Copyright © 2010 23 Kazoos, LLC

Printed in the United States of America.

Kenney, Wendy.

How to Build Buzz for Your Biz

Tap into the Power of Social Media, Publicity and Relationship Marketing to Grow Your Business

ISBN: 978-0-9844034-1-7

Cover Design and Layout by Monkey Graphics

WARNING: Disclaimer

The purpose of the book is to educate and entertain. The author/ publisher does not guarantee that anyone following the techniques, suggestions, tips, ideas, or strategies will become rich, famous or wealthy. The author/publisher shall have neither liability nor responsibility to anyone with respect to any loss or damage caused, or alleged to be caused, directly or indirectly by the information contained in this book.

Dedication

This book is dedicated to small business owners everywhere.
Here's to your success!

TABLE OF CONTENTS

INTRODUCTION

I'm sure you've noticed it yourself: traditional advertising is dying. The death of newspaper and television advertising, and direct mail is evidenced by the demise of newspapers like the *Chicago Sun-Times* and the *Rocky Mountain News* in 2009. It's no wonder that traditional advertising doesn't stand a chance. Who can keep track of one company's slogan amidst the barrage? The average person gets inundated by as many as 3,000 advertising messages a day. We can barely remember what we read two paragraphs ago, let alone recall an ad we saw a day ago. So if you think you can just put an ad in the newspaper or send out a few mailers with the result that people will flock to your business, you're dead wrong! Believe me: many companies go out of business every day because of that mistaken approach.

Getting customers is a business owner's biggest dilemma and greatest responsibility. As a business owner, you can have the best product or service in the world, but that means nothing if you don't get the word out about what you're offering.

So how do you find customers? How do you put out your messages? How do you get people talking so they spread the word on your behalf?

You'll find the answers to those questions and more in these pages. This book is all about finding and keeping new customers. Each of the strategies you'll learn here have been implemented with great success–they helped transform my own business from a small start-up into a six-figure gold mine in less than 12 months.

AND IF I CAN DO IT, SO CAN YOU.

I started my company, 23 Kazoos, LLC, in 2009, after almost seven years in the financial services industry as a financial advisor who assisted clients with their investment and life insurance needs. It was a tough decision for me to leave the comfort of my steady job because I'd developed many relationships over the years and had hundreds of clients, most of whom had become my friends. But I was also miserable.

I had always dreamed of writing and speaking professionally, and after seven years in the financial industry, I knew it wasn't going to happen because of the strict regulations on securities representatives. In addition, the demands of the industry did not leave much time to pursue my creative desires. The stress of long hours and the constant pressure to sell financial products to earn my commissions became unbearable, affecting my health and my relationships. I knew I had to make a change.

And so I took a leap of faith. I decided that if I could succeed at selling life insurance, what I consider to be one of the most difficult industries in the world, I could sell anything. In April 2009, 23 Kazoos, LLC was born.

Since then it's been an incredible and fun roller coaster ride: I've had the opportunity to speak to groups and associations about marketing; I've helped dozens of fabulous companies with marketing strategies and we've had some extraordinary results.

In this book you'll learn about some of the strategies that I've used to build buzz for many businesses. You'll find out the biggest marketing mistake that most businesses make, and how to avoid it; you'll discover how I got 9,000 visitors to my website in just one day; and you'll learn exactly where to go and which marketing strategies I've used to find new customers.

And the most useful thing you'll learn is how to do all of these things for little or no cash.

Advertising may be dying, but marketing is very much alive and thriving via social media, publicity and relationship-building. Tap into the power of these tools and you'll soon see the results! The marketing strategies in this book will help you generate buzz for your company, attract new customers and get even more business, all without breaking the bank.

WENDY NELSON KENNEY

23 Kazoos, LLC

WNKenney@23Kazoos.com

www.23Kazoos.com

www.HowToBuildBuzzForYourBiz.com

http://www.twitter.com/wendykenney

http://facebook.com/23Kazoos

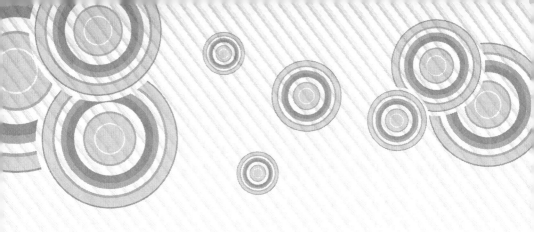

SECTION ONE

BACK TO THE BASICS: BUILDING YOUR BUSINESS MARKETING PLAN

Most people wouldn't build a house with only a screwdriver or stir their coffee with a hammer, but too many business owners jump right in to marketing without having the proper tools in place for the job.

And one of the most important tools you can have is a *plan* ...

CHAPTER 1

WHO'S YOUR IDEAL CUSTOMER?

My husband collects baseball caps and at one time had at least 50 in his closet. If I asked to borrow one, he'd look at me, shrug his shoulders and say, "Which one?" But if I asked to borrow a *specific* baseball cap, such as a red one, or an Ohio State cap, he knew exactly which one I was after.

The same is true in business. The more specific you can be in identifying your ideal customer, the one you most want to attract, the more successful you'll be in your business. It's that easy.

HOW DO YOU IDENTIFY YOUR IDEAL CLIENT?

Probably the easiest way to pinpoint your ideal customer is to study your existing client base. Then answer the following questions with your client base in mind. (If you're just starting your business and don't have any clients yet, answer these questions by thinking about the types of clients you'd *like* to attract.) Is there a certain "type" of customer who represents the majority of your client base (e.g., young business owners, bankers, etc.)? What do your clients have in common? Who do you enjoy working with the most? What about the least?

One business owner I know in the insurance industry discovered that his ideal clients all owned storage units. He enjoyed working with these clients because he, too, had a background in the storage industry having worked in a storage unit that was owned by his family.

In addition, he shared many of the same values with these clients, such as family, independence and hard work. The business owner found that because he connected with these *other* business owners on so many different levels, they had excellent rapport. They became his best sales force!

THE BUSINESS OWNER DOUBLED HIS INCOME IN ONLY A FEW YEARS

How did he do it? First and foremost, he focused his energy on two or three types of ideal customers instead of trying to be all things to all people. He used some of the other marketing strategies outlined in this book to make himself visible to those two or three groups and became known to them as a friend, colleague and advocate. As they got to know him, his ideal clients began to buy from him and refer their friends in the industry. It was a very successful way to grow his business.

My ideal customers are highly creative, busy, independent business owners who value the expertise of other professionals. Because I have had a lifelong love affair with food, and got my start in the restaurant industry, I especially enjoy working with local, independent restaurant owners.

But all of my ideal clients share the same characteristics of having family values, passion for excellence and creativity, and vision.

The exercise below will help you to discover who your ideal client is. Knowing your ideal client will help you throughout this book as you develop the best marketing plan for your business.

ACTION STEPS:

Who are your ideal customers that you have worked with in the past or are working with now? List them by name here:

_____

_____

_____

What characteristics do these people have in common with you?

_____

_____

_____

Why do you enjoy working with them?

_____

_____

_____

What characteristics do these clients have in common with each other? You could consider points such as their values, hobbies and demographics.

_____

_____

_____

How do these clients gather information when they have a problem to solve? Do they ask for referrals? Do they go to the Internet?

_____

_____

_____

Do these clients use social media? If so, which platforms do they use? Twitter, LinkedIn, Facebook or any others? Do they have blogs?

_____

_____

_____

What television and radio stations do they like?

_____

_____

_____

CHAPTER 2

Give 'Em What They Want, When They Want It

Now that you've formed a better idea of who your ideal customers are, you need to identify *how* you can meet their desires. So let's look at a few examples of businesses that have profited by aptly answering to their customers *wants*.

Joe's Real BBQ: Known from Coast to Coast

One of my favorite restaurants is Joe's Real BBQ, (www.JoesReal-BBQ.com) owned by Joe Johnston and Tad Peelen in Gilbert, Arizona. Joe's Real BBQ has been a Phoenix area favorite since 1998.

Customers come back again and again, bringing their families and out of town guests to eat the melt-in-your mouth barbecue pork, ham and ribs. Joe's Real BBQ has won "Best Barbecue" from the *Arizona Republic* and *Phoenix New Times* for several years, and has been featured in numerous publications such as *Sunset Magazine*. It was also nominated for the "Best Brisket" on the nationally syndicated *Live with Regis and Kelly* television show.

So What Makes Joe's Real BBQ Restaurant Stand Out from the Crowd?

Joe Johnston and Tad Peelen understand what their customers want and they deliver.

Joe attributes the restaurant's success to four things. According to Joe:

"We are wired to:

(1) *be the best,*

(2) *never compromise on quality, even if it is difficult,*

(3) *to go deep in the process (know as much and control as much as possible) and*

(4) *enjoy people and relationships."*[1]

The owners of Joe's Real BBQ actively engage with their customers in person and via social media every day. They gather valuable feedback to find out what their customers *want*. Then they do something amazing: they give it to them.

Want Versus Need

According to Dictionary.com, *want* is defined as the following:

1. to feel a need or a desire for; wish for: *to want one's dinner; always wanting something new.*

2. to wish, need, crave, demand, or desire.

"Needs" are defined as being requirements, necessary duties or obligations. I need food; I need transportation; I need to pay my cell phone bill.

"Wants" are driven by our emotions, and sometimes those emotions are very strong. Needs may or may not be emotion-driven.

What's the Difference Between My Seven-Year-Old Granddaughter Crying for a Toy in Walmart and Your Customers? Absolutely Nothing!

In Walmart one day with her mother, my granddaughter, Sarah, who was at the time seven years old, saw a toy that she wanted. When her mother wouldn't buy it for her, Sarah suddenly erupted into a crying spell; her heart was broken. Her mother offered to make a deal with Sarah to allow her to earn the toy, and Sarah's *want* for the toy was so strong, that she accepted.

The point is that, like Sarah, as a customer not only do I want what I *want,* I want it *when* I want it—which is usually now. I don't mean any offense here, but as adults we're no different than children. The difference is that as adults we have more access to get what we want when we want it!

Many experts say that you should give your customers what they need. But forget about that. If her mom had offered Sarah toothpaste she would *not* have wanted it, even though she has a need for it daily. The same is true with our customers. What kid (or adult) wants what he or she needs? Not me! I don't want what I need, I want what I *want!* Yes, as a customer, I'm very much like a child.

Sometimes my wants correlate with my needs, sometimes they don't. But timing is everything. And for me the time is always right now!

WHAT PEOPLE WANT DURING A RECESSION

The last few years will go down in the history books as the years of the second greatest economic crisis in American history. Maybe you've been affected directly. Unemployment has been as high 10 percent[2], but in my house, the unemployment rate rose to 50 percent when my spouse was laid off for over a year. His layoff hit our family hard. What once was a two-income family had been suddenly thrust into single-income status and we found ourselves making some very hard financial decisions: just like countless other families in America.

On top of nationwide layoffs, the stock market took a huge nose dive and with it the retirement savings of thousands of people, including me.

So, like many American households, providing for our family and surviving financially has been at the top of our minds. We ruthlessly cut out every extra expenditure, including eating out. But that wasn't what we *wanted* to do. We *wanted* to continue living our lives just like we had been!

HOW MCDONALD'S IS GIVING PEOPLE WHAT THEY WANT WHEN THEY WANT IT

Up stepped McDonald's with some phenomenal marketing campaigns. It introduced 99-cent, large-sized soft drinks during the summer, and then it expanded the offer to include any-sized soft drinks and coffee.

Later, McDonald's amped up its dollar menu to include breakfast. Suddenly, eating out wasn't the expensive proposition that it used to be!

Up to this point, I hadn't been to a McDonald's in years. But its marketing campaigns certainly got my attention. How could I resist taking my three teenage sons out to eat again for less than the cost of a pizza? McDonald's gave me what I wanted!

In addition, McDonald's many restaurants have been remodeled to reflect a more adult-friendly comfort, including the new McCafé which offers a premium cup of coffee at prices much lower than those in McDonald's coffee house competitors.

As a business owner, I frequently hold business meetings in local coffee houses, but before McCafé, I was feeling the pinch of those coffee house prices. With the launch of McCafé, I can have my business meetings in a very comfortable environment and pay less than one dollar to boot! *And* their coffee is good!

It's because McDonald's is giving me and millions of others worldwide what we want that it's one of the best marketing organizations in the world. For years, McDonald's has been able to provide customers food, experiences, services and prices that they want, and in doing so, it has been able to continue producing profits while many of its competitors struggle.

McDonald's marketing approach has clearly been a success. At a time when sales in the fast food industry were down overall, McDonald's experienced a 3.3 percent growth in global sales. The corporation's CEO, Jim Skinner, sums it up perfectly:

"Our customers are at the heart of everything we do, and McDonald's is delivering what they want."

THE FINAL WORD: GIVE 'EM WHAT THEY WANT

As a business owner, I've learned that my business is not about a specific product or service. It's about giving customers what they want. And as a customer, what I want is number one on my mind! I want to have fun, feel better, look better, make more money, spend less money, have better relationships–and I want all the methods for arriving at these results to be quick and easy. It's all about what I want right now!

Do I need a fancy cup of coffee? No, but I *want* it, and in this world of short-term, quick fix, instant satisfaction, I'm going to get what I want when I want it. The difference between a good economy and a bad economy however, might mean that now I want to pay less for that cup of coffee.

But it's not always about price; it's also about what customers value. So if you can't offer the rock bottom prices that McDonald's can, what you *can* do is to offer amazing service and a memorable experience in other ways.

WHAT *YOUR* CUSTOMERS WANT

Are you listening to your customers? Do you know what they want? Have you even asked?

Before you start to market your business, the steps below will help you to answer the question: "What is it that your ideal customers really *want?*"

ACTION STEPS:

What are your ideal customers buying from your competitors?

_____

_____

_____

Why are your ideal customers buying from your competitors?

_____

_____

_____

What do your customers want in regard to your product or service offering? For example, if you own a car dealership, are the buyers buying cars based on price, gas mileage, looks, size or other factors?

_____

_____

_____

Are you providing what your ideal customers want? If not, how can you?

_____

_____

_____

FOOTNOTES:

1. Johnston, Joe. "A Brief History of the Coffee Plantation - Part 4." Roaster Project. 1 April 2010. Web. 5 May 2010. http://www.roasterproject.com/2010/04/a-brief-history-of-the-coffee-plantation-part-4/

2. Trading Economics. "United States Unemployment Rate." Trading Economics. 2 April 2010. Web. 5 May 2010. http://www.tradingeconomics.com/Economics/Unemployment-rate.aspx?Symbol=USD

CHAPTER 3

GIRLS (AND BOYS) JUST WANNA HAVE FUN: ADDING VALUE TO THE EXPERIENCE

It's during tough economic times that people want–no, they desperately crave–experiences that help them feel better. They want authenticity; they want to know that people care for them; they want to feel secure and comfortable with their buying decisions.

SPICE UP YOUR CLIENTS' *WANTS* WITH SOME ADDED VALUE

To grow your business in a down economy, or any economy, you need to do more than just "dare to be different." You need to delight people with difference and caress them with caring. Your customers have many choices, and in order for them to choose you, you must give them more value than your competitors!

What do your ideal customers value? If they're like most people, they want someone to help them feel better about themselves or their situation. Do you make them laugh? Do you add an element of surprise?

It's All About the Experience

My husband and I have frequented our favorite taco shop, Guedo's, in Chandler, Arizona, for over 20 years. Every time we walk in the door, we enjoy the same familiar experience: we smell the tender and flavorful marinated meats cooking on the grill, and that wonderful scent pulls us right in!

The servers greet us by name and take our order, the usual: two savory, marinated, grilled, mixed steak and pork tacos on fresh corn tortillas with melted cheese. We top it all off at the salsa bar that features homemade and authentic salsas made with freshly chopped ingredients. Every time we eat there, we agree that the tacos are the best we've ever eaten. **Why has Guedo's become our favorite? The biggest reason: the experience.** And it's an experience we have consistently enjoyed for over ten years.

Once you've created that special experience for your customers, they'll grow to expect it and look forward to it (like we do every time we go to Guedo's). Then you can consider shaking things up by creating new or unusual experiences. Guedo's does this by offering new and different menu items, while still maintaining the same fabulous atmosphere.

Keep your customers guessing about what exciting twists will come next. Delight them with difference, caress them with caring. And trust me that they'll keep buzzing about it to the people they know (*and* they'll keep coming back for more!).

ACTION STEPS:

What kind of experience does your business provide?

_____

_____

_____

Is your staff friendly and caring?

_____

_____

_____

Do you know your customers by name?

_____

_____

_____

Do you respond quickly to calls, problems and requests?

_____

_____

_____

Do you provide consistency in your service and your product offerings? How?

_____

_____

_____

Are you known for quality?

_____

_____

_____

How do you delight people with difference and caress them with caring?

_____

_____

_____

CHAPTER 4

How to Reach Your Ideal Customers Now That You Know What They Want

So you've figured out who your ideal customers are and what they want right now.

Now the million dollar question: How do you reach them? How do you get the word out that you have the answers to the wants that people have?

The simple answer is: it depends. I know, it's probably not as simple as you'd hoped. But hear me out.

There are many methods for reaching potential customers, but the best way is the way that they prefer to communicate and gather information. Let's look at the research to see how the people in your ideal client groups prefer to get information.

Research has shown that people who fall into certain demographic groups have a more preferred way of gathering information.

The Media Your Customers Use

Baby boomers (born 1946-1964) make up 32.5 percent of the American adult population and 36 percent of the adult online population, according to the Pew Internet & American Life Project.[1] Based on one study of baby boomers, nearly two thirds (62.6 percent) of the people in this age group spend more than five hours a week online.[2]

However, baby boomers still read newspapers and watch television news. They are not traditionally "early adopters," meaning they wait until everyone else has tried something before trying it themselves. Now that social media is past its infancy stages, however, boomers are adopting social media in droves. Indeed, Facebook has reported that boomers represent the fastest growing demographic in terms of adoption.[3]

Generation Xers (born 1965-1980) have the fastest growing social media adoption rate of all age groups. It's estimated that over 90 percent of Generation Xers are online. In fact, they are considered to be the most fragmented users of media because they practice a wider range of lifestyles than previous generations.[4]

Millennials/Generation Yers (born 1981-2001) are the first generation to grow up with Internet access. Computers were part of their educational experience, and as a result, they are very comfortable with technology. Over 91 percent of millennials use the Internet. Generally, they are the first to adopt social media platforms like MySpace and Facebook.

People born in the Generation Y period are the biggest users of text messaging, many preferring texting over actually talking on the phone. They are the least likely to read print media such as newspapers and magazines.

Demographic Research Has Huge Implications for Business Owners

For example: we know that people over the age of 45 are the biggest consumers of newspaper media, while, on the majority, people under the age of 35 rarely read the newspaper at all. Those in age ranges of up to 35 years tend to prefer the Internet as their medium of choice when they're looking for solutions to their *want* problems.[5]

With all of the previous information in mind, you can start to see the types of media that your ideal customers prefer to use, and therefore which media you should use for marketing to them.

Another way to find out your ideal customers' preferred method of interaction is to simply ask them. You can send them a survey via e-mail using Survey Monkey (http://www.surveymonkey.com). Or you can simply call them and ask them questions such as the following:

- Do you use social media?

- Do you frequently use e-mail?

- Do you like to use texting?

- Are you the type of person who rushes to the mailbox every day?

Whatever the preferred method of communication is for your ideal clients, you must use it to reach them. In many cases, however, you will need to use multiple methods. Answer the following questions to gain a better idea of the best ways to reach your clients.

ACTION STEPS:

In an earlier action step, you listed your current ideal clients by name and determined what they have in common. Now you will list the characteristics that they have in common.

For example, I discovered that one of my current classifications of ideal customers are independent business owners/entrepreneurs who own a restaurant or a highly creative and unique business. Each of the business owners/entrepreneurs in this group have an excellent product, and quality and service are very important to them.

List one of your ideal customer types based on common characteristics they share. For instance, based on the example above, I would write "Independent restaurant owners."

_____

_____

_____

What do the people in this ideal customer group do in their spare time? What are their hobbies and interests?

_____

_____

_____

Who do they hang out with?

_____

_____

_____

What is a typical business day like for the people in this ideal customer group?

_____

_____

_____

Where do the people in this group go first when they have a problem, whether business-related or otherwise, that needs to be solved?

_____

_____

_____

What media do the people in this ideal customer group prefer? Do they like to watch television news or read the newspaper?

_____

_____

_____

Do the people in this group use social media? If so, which platforms do they use?

_____

_____

_____

Footnotes:

1. Pew Internet. "Baby Boomers and the Internet." *Pew Internet*. 14 November 2002. Web. 5 May 2010. http://www.pewinternet.org/Press-Releases/2002/Baby-Boomers-and-the-Internet.aspx

2. Phillips, Lisa E. "Boomer Demographics and Media Usage." *eMarketer*. January 2010. Web. 5 May 2010. http://www.emarketer.com/Report.aspx?code=emarketer_2000640

3. The Cline Group. "Baby Boomers and Matures: Fastest Growing Group on the Social Web." 1 February 2010. Web. 5 May 2010. http://www.facebook.com/note.php?note_id=280285850185

4. eMarketer. "Where Is Generation X?" *eMarketer*. 3 November 2008. Web. 5 May 2010. http://www.emarketer.com/Article.aspx?R=1006699

5. Newspaper Audience. "Who Is Reading: A Question of Demographics." *Journalism*. 13 March 2006. Web. 5 May 2010. http://www.journalism.org/node/639

CHAPTER 5

GETTING CUSTOMERS IS EASY WITH YOUR MARKETING GPS

You've identified your ideal customers, you know their wants, and now you've also developed an idea of the best places to reach them with marketing. Now let's start putting together a workable plan.

"VISIBILITY + CREDIBILITY = PROFITABILITY"

Ivan Misner, the founder of BNI (Business Networking International) teaches that *"Visibility + Credibility = Profitability."* The key to building a successful marketing plan is that your potential customers have to see you everywhere and frequently (in a positive way, of course).

So how do you map out the marketing plan that will get you the visibility and credibility that you need?

LET'S TALK ABOUT GLOBAL POSITIONING SYSTEMS

I heard once that people who get lost easily are geniuses. I don't know if that's true or not, but I do know that without current direction-giving technology, I would get lost almost every time I drive somewhere new!

One of my favorite modern day tools is my portable Tom Tom global positioning system (GPS). I simply enter my destination, and the amazing little machine tells me how to get there, turn-by-turn, in the quickest way possible. This technology is a huge time and money saver for millions of people: there's no more need to ask for directions, or to potentially get lost and arrive at a destination late and frustrated.

YOUR MARKETING GPS

As a business owner, I have a tendency to get sidetracked, which wastes time and money. This has made having my own personal marketing plan or "marketing GPS" very valuable.

Until someone invents a portable, small business marketing GPS system, we have to figure out our marketing approach manually. And that's why I created the 10-Minute Marketing Plan™, the simple system that I have used with each of my clients, and with which I've had amazing results.

THE 10-MINUTE MARKETING PLAN™

Have you heard the phrase "multiple streams of income?" In marketing, you need to have multiple streams of *prospects*. The 10-Minute Marketing Plan™ helps you to grow your visibility, and subsequently your profitability, by outlining marketing strategies that will help you tap into multiple streams of prospects.

How It Works

The 10-Minute Marketing Plan™ is based on a simple process of outlining 10 consistent marketing strategies that you can employ on a quarterly basis to fill your business pipeline.

Quarterly planning is key because marketing takes time. The marketing that you implement this quarter will begin to fill your pipeline in the next quarter.

The plan focuses on the four seasons of the year, which are each natural evaluation points for your business. Enacting a particular marketing plan for one season gives you time to evaluate what's working and what's not working, and to adjust accordingly. Furthermore, a strategy that works one season might not work in all of them. This is a simple and effective way to plan your small business marketing strategy.

Your Annual Marketing Goals

In order to put together your own 10-Minute Marketing Plan™ you next need to outline your marketing goals for the year.

Write down your annual goals in terms of the following:

1. The number of new clients that you'd like to bring in

2. The amount of money that you intend to generate through sales

3. Your total intended revenue dollars

4. Your reward goals, such as taking a much-needed vacation

Now let's start to assemble your own 10-Minute Marketing Plan™. I want you to fold down the corner of this page so that you can keep coming back to it. As you read through this book and learn more about the marketing strategies available to you, come back here to finish or update your list of the 10 strategies you want to use regularly for your company. This should be where you record the points in this book that you most want to try out for yourself.

ACTION STEPS:

List 10 marketing strategies that you would like to use on a regular basis to market your company (such as Twitter, Facebook, e-mail marketing, networking groups, blogging, freebie offers, publicity, etc.).

Note: For a list of 101 Marketing Activities go to www.HowtoBuildBuzzforYourBiz.com

1. _____

2. _____

3. _____

4. _____

5. _____

6. _____

7. _____

8. _____

9. _____

10. _____

What are your marketing goals for next season?

_____

_____

_____

What holidays or special events are occurring in the next season that will be at the top of your customers' minds?

_____

_____

_____

CHAPTER 6

THE BIG MARKETING MISTAKE BUSINESS OWNERS MAKE AND HOW TO AVOID IT

Have you ever had this happen to you?

Several years ago, I attended a business networking function and I just happened to strike up a conversation with a person who sold cars for a local Chevrolet dealership.

And as luck would have it, I was in the market for a new car and was especially looking for a Chevrolet Trailblazer. I really liked the person with whom I was speaking. I told them that I was in the market for a Chevy and asked if they would contact me. We exchanged business cards and I looked forward to their call.

Well, a few days passed, and I hadn't heard from the salesperson. I was very anxious because I really wanted to get myself into a new Trailblazer. So I gave them a call, leaving a voice message on their cell phone and on their office phone. And then I waited for a return call. Then I waited some more. After a few days with still no word from the salesperson, I finally gave up.

Hey, if they didn't want my business, I could take my money somewhere else. In the end, I bought my Trailblazer through my credit union's car buying service.

I've had this happen to me several times. In each case, the sales person or business owner has lost *thousands of dollars* in sales from me – all because they didn't follow up!

Marketing Is *Not* the Same as Selling

Many business owners confuse the term "marketing" with the term "selling." Marketing is simply the process or strategies you use to get the word out about your business and gather leads. Selling is the process of turning those leads into paying customers.

This is the biggest problem I see in marketing: you can be the best marketer in the world, but if you don't convert the leads to clients *you have nothing*. And the most important step in converting leads to clients is simply following up with them. (Note the word "simply." It's really that easy!)

Follow Up and Reap the Rewards!

There are many ways to follow up with leads or prospects; here are just three:

1. **Phone:** After you exchange information and agree to follow up, give your lead a call within 24 hours. Say something like, "Hey, I said I would follow up with you, and here I am! I would love to get together with you to learn more about your needs." Don't make it your goal to sell them your prod-

uct over the phone. Aim to set an appointment and build a relationship. Find out about what they want before you start selling them.

2. **E-Mail:** If the thought of making a phone call gives you hives, then you can also follow up by e-mail. The benefit to e-mail is that you can do it any time, and your lead can answer at their convenience. If you don't hear back from them though, go back to step one.

3. **Snail Mail:** Yes, snail mail still exists, and believe it or not, people enjoy getting old fashioned cards and letters. If you're just not sure about the lead, or if you want to send them some additional information, sending a letter via regular mail is a good option. Of course, if the contact has indicated that they're looking to make a purchase ASAP, don't use snail mail. Give 'em a call first: within 24 hours is best.

The Failure to Follow Up Is the Biggest Mistake Small Business Owners Make

---

It ends up costing businesses thousands, if not millions, of dollars. Don't let this happen to you! Follow up with people right away. **I guarantee your sales will soar!**

Now that you've started putting your marketing strategy in place, remember this rule as you become acquainted with many new potential clients.

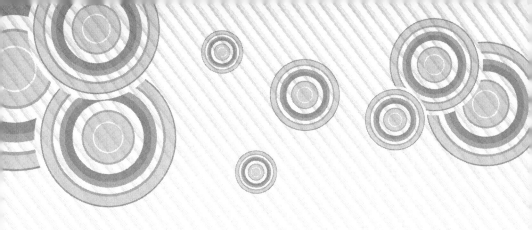

SECTION TWO

SOCIAL MEDIA MARKETING

CHAPTER 7

How to Use Social Media to Build Buzz for Your Business

Social media has changed the face of marketing forever. What was once a one-way message pushed from the company to the consumer has become a two-way conversation, requiring both parties to participate. Now your customers have a voice in the marketplace and their voices are loud and clear.

One study showed that an unhappy customer tells 11 people about their bad experience with a business.[1] But that was before social media. I have more than 5,500 followers on Twitter, and 800 friends on Facebook, not to mention hundreds of followers on other social networks. If I'm not happy with a business, I have the ability to get the word out to thousands of people!

Because of the ease with which millions of people are now able to communicate with their hundreds of friends in mere seconds, social media or social networking is fast becoming a marketing powerhouse for many businesses. Not only that, but social media sites are also excellent places for businesses to meet potential virtual team members.

SOCIAL MEDIA: WHAT'S IT ALL ABOUT?

Social media comes in many different forms including social networks such as LinkedIn, Facebook or MySpace; online forums such as Meetup; micro-blogging platforms such as Twitter or Google Buzz; social newsrooms such as Digg, Reddit, StumbleUpon or Yahoo! Buzz; and photo sharing sites such as Flickr or Picasa.

There are even social media sites for online video sharing, including YouTube and Vimeo.

But the term "social media" also includes blogs, dynamic websites, optimized press releases and case studies, e-books, online magazines, white papers, Internet radio shows, Internet television shows and podcasts.

Basically, social media is anything that relies on person-to-person interaction to share information.

The beauty of social media platforms is that they are opt-in, meaning that people choose to receive communication from you by opting in to follow you or be your fan. This presents a huge opportunity: no longer is your communication limited to current customers. As long as people remain members of your social media networks, they can receive your messages days, months or even years after they've used your services.

Why *Your* Business Should Use Social Media Marketing

Social media has so many amazing benefits, but probably the biggest for small businesses is that it enables them to reach a much larger audience in a much shorter period of time than what typical advertising permits (unless, of course, you've got millions to blow on publicity!). For this reason, social media has become a very effective, low-cost marketing tool when it's used the right way.

With social media, you can create new relationships, strengthen existing ones and leverage your time. You can even research your market, find your ideal customers and brand yourself.

When used properly, social media becomes a form of inbound marketing–every business owner's dream. Suddenly clients are calling you because they've heard about you. Gone are the days of forceful advertising that leave you feeling like a sleazy telemarketer: you don't have to push your company on anyone. Instead, let *them* come to *you*.

What Social Marketing Is Doing for Other Businesses

In the short time that social media has been around it has helped business owners do the following:

- Reach people who were previously difficult to reach

- Build new relationships with target consumers

- Improve website search engine rankings

- Create visibility and credibility, which equals profitability

- Monitor the environment to more quickly adjust to consumer needs and wants

- Improve satisfaction

- Keep up with the competition

Regardless of whether you use social media as a marketing tool, it is impacting your business right now. Your customers are talking about you whether you like it or not! It's essential to the success of your business that you continually monitor the social media environment. Find out what people are saying about you so that you can respond appropriately and quickly.

So you'd better jump on the bandwagon and become a part of the conversation–before it's too late!

Footnotes:

1. Griffin, Jill. "One Unhappy Customer Can Multiply to Many." *Austin Business Journal*. 19 March 1999. Web. 5 May 2010. http://www.bizjournals.com/austin/stories/1999/03/22/smallb3.html

.

CHAPTER 8

Knowing Where to Begin

So you've astutely decided to use social media marketing as part of your publicity strategy. Congratulations! This marks the beginning of a more exciting, more involved and more rewarding marketing path for your business.

Now it's time to decide which type of social media to use. There are so many to pick from that the social media newbie can easily get overwhelmed.

_ONDE MNDM EM

Where Do You Start?

The simple answer: start with your "ideal customer." Once you know which platforms your ideal customers use, you'll know where to focus your social media marketing.

In Chapter 1 you identified your ideal clients. Now take a second to bring a picture of your ideal customer to mind, then answer these questions:

1. How old are they?

2. Are they male or female?

3. What's their annual household income?

4. Are they college educated?

Once you've answered these questions, you have everything you need to find out which social media platforms they use, and therefore where you need to create your business's presence. Keeping the traits of your ideal customer in mind, take a look at three of the most popular social media platforms used by businesses:

LinkedIn

- Average user age: 41[1]

- 64 percent are male[1]

- Average income: $109,000[1]

- 80 percent are college grads[1]

Does this sound like your ideal customer? If so, then you should be using LinkedIn, which has more than 65 million active users[2], to promote your business.

Twitter

- Average user age: 39[3]

- 55 percent are female[4]

- 58 percent make over $60,000 per year[4]

- 51 percent are college grads[4]

Facebook

- Average user age: 38[3]

- 54 percent are female[5]

- Average income: around $60,000[6]

- Average user has no college education[7]

Do these sound like your ideal customer? Then you might want to engage with them through Twitter and Facebook.

As you see, Twitter and Facebook have much in common, although Twitter appears to appeal to the educated community more so than Facebook. With more than 105 million Twitter users[8], and over 400 million Facebook users[9], either platform has the potential for reaching huge numbers.

While LinkedIn, Twitter and Facebook platforms are used for business connections and networking, LinkedIn caters more toward the professional audience. It serves as a virtual online resume and testimonial bank. Facebook, however, leans almost purely toward extracurricular social interaction.

"Friends" on Facebook can play games□ such as the wildly popular "FarmVille" and "Mafia Wars"□ with one another. They can also send each other birthday wishes and virtual gifts. If Facebook is where your ideal customers are, check out the games, join groups, be active in existing forums (or create your own), post comments about other businesses and ask for testimonials for yours.

Which social media platform should you use? Eventually you can use all of them and reach a variety of different people. But to make it easy, just start with the platform that your current clients use. If the demographic study we just did didn't help you identify which platform they use, pick up the phone, or send an e-mail to your existing ideal clients and find out where they spend time on social networks.

Now, let's consider some social marketing strategy.

FOOTNOTES:

1. Schonfeld, Erick. "LinkedIn to Launch Its Own Ad Network." *Tech Crunch*. 14 September 2008. Web. 5 May 2010. http://techcrunch.com/2008/09/14/linkedin-to-launch-its-own-ad-network/

2. LinkedIn. Homepage. *LinkedIn*. Web. 5 May 2010. http://www.linkedin.com/

3. Pingdom. "Study: Ages of Social Network Users." *Royal Pingdom*. 16 February 2010. Web. 5 May 2010. http://royal.pingdom.com/2010/02/16/study-ages-of-social-network-users/

4. Quantcast. "Monthly Traffic: Twitter.com." *Quantcast*. Web. 5 May 2010. http://www.quantcast.com/twitter.com

5. Smith, Justin. "Latest Data on US Facebook Age and Gender Demographics." *Inside Facebook*. 18 September 2008. Web. 5 May 2010. http://www.insidefacebook.com/2008/09/18/latest-data-on-us-facebook-age-and-gender-demographics/

6. Anand. "Income Levels of MySpace and Facebook Users." *Tech Crunchies*. 3 December 2008. Web. 5 May 2010. http://gorumors.com/crunchies/income-levels-of-myspace-and-facebook-users/

7. Alexa. "Facebook.com: Audience." *Alexa*. Web. 5 May 2010. http://www.alexa.com/siteinfo/facebook.com#

8. Bosker, Bianca. "Twitter User Statistics Revealed." *The Huffington Post*. 30 April 2010. Web. 5 May 2010. http://www.huffingtonpost.com/2010/04/14/twitter-user-statistics-r_n_537992.html

9. Facebook. "Press Room." *Facebook*. Web. 5 May 2010. http://www.facebook.com/press/info.php?statistics

CHAPTER 9

YOUR SOCIAL MEDIA MARKETING STRATEGY

STEP 1: SET YOUR GOALS

Goals are important because, first and foremost, they allow you to be upfront with the people in your Internet communities about why you are there. And if you're upfront with your reasons for being involved in social marketing, then your customers will respect and trust you for your honesty. Trust is key for finding and maintaining clients.

Ask yourself what are your goals: Do you want to get new customers? Are you using social media to create visibility and credibility? Or are you there to service your customers? Your goals can be endless.

For example, selling on social media is an acceptable goal, but only if you state what you're doing upfront. Amazon has a Twitter account just for Amazon Deals (http://twitter.com/amazondeals). Amazon Deals has over 40,000 followers and all it does is post "Lightening Deals" from Amazon.

But unless you're a retail business that is known for great deals or low prices, I don't recommend having a Twitter account just to sell. Keep in mind that social media is social first. Just like you wouldn't go to a party and push your business cards on people before you introduce yourself, neither should you push your business on social media. People need to get to know you first. Blatantly advertising your products will only alienate you in the eyes of your followers, who may label you as a spammer. Don't do it. You'll cause serious damage to your credibility.

For most small businesses, your initial goal should be: **create visibility and establish new relationships; then the sales will follow**.

What if your company is already very visible like Amazon? In that case, you might have a goal of **increasing sales; and then it would be appropriate to have a Twitter account just for that purpose. But remember, you've got to state your purpose up front, in the profile of your Twitter account**.

Once you've established the purpose of using social media in your business marketing, you must communicate this in writing to your employees. You can do this by creating a Social Media Policy for your business. This should be a document that outlines the parameters of social media use in your company. In it, you need to define who will use your business's social media; what types of messages are allowed and what types are not; what types of platforms will be used and how often.

Why is it so important to clearly delineate the purpose(s) and method(s) of your social marketing campaign? Because establishing the guidelines ahead of time can save your company a lot of headache and heartache in the long run! In fact, you can actually get into trouble with the law if you don't represent yourself honestly on social media platforms! The Federal Trade Commission recently passed new disclosure laws requiring that anyone who provides testimonials for products and services via social media as part of a paid relationship must disclose that relationship. Before you get started, take some time to familiarize yourself with the laws regarding social media marketing, and consult your attorney for more information. http://www.ftc.gov/opa/2009/10/endortest.shtm

Intel Corporation (http://www.intcl.com) is one of the pioneers in constructing social media policy. And although your company may not be as big as Intel, their policy is a good place to garner ideas about how to get started. You can access Intel's social media policy here: http://www.intel.com/sites/sitewide/en_US/social-media.htm.

STEP 2: MAKE FRIENDS WITH THE BIG BOYS

Obviously you're here to use social marketing to reach future clients. But **you also want to use social media to spark new relationships with people in the media, individuals who have influence because of their large followings and potential referral partners.** All of these are invaluable resources because they have the ability to tell many people about your business.

You need to intentionally follow people who fit these categories. Before they can become a part of your social network, you must become a part of theirs. *Sure*, you say. *If I knew people in the media, I'd already have it made.* Well, there are many ways to find people in each of these categories, even if you've never rubbed elbows with them before.

Twitter is a good place to start because you can use the "Find People" tab to locate people by name. You can also use the "Search" box to search for people by key words.

Let's say you own a local retail store or restaurant. You'd type in the street name and city where your store is located, then follow the people you find who meet your ideal customer criteria.

The question is: "How do I find followers? People who follow me?" Well, the unwritten etiquette on Twitter is that if you follow people first, they will follow you back. However, that's only if they are interested in what you have to say, which gives you another good reason not to sell on Twitter.

There are also a host of third party tools that can help you find people to follow on Twitter. Check out Appendix A for some of my favorites.

STEP 3: JUMP IN AND GET INVOLVED!

Yes, you should definitely use social media to keep in contact with clients and strengthen relationships. But you also need to use it to increase visibility and credibility. How do you do this? By being truly engaged in your social media platforms.

Customers and prospects expect you to be engaged. If someone makes a comment about you or your company, good or bad, it's important that you respond. You wouldn't ignore someone who called you up and told you how great your service is, would you? (Please say, *No*.)

Notice I didn't say that people *want* you to be engaged, but that they *expect* it of you. Social media has become a new platform for customer service, and in order to deliver the best service possible, your business must engage with its customers regardless of whatever else you've got going on. If you don't respond and engage, it's assumed that you don't care. And if you don't care about your customers, they most certainly won't care about you.

LET'S CREATE SOME ACCOUNTS!

So let's give this a shot. We'll start with Twitter. Create a Twitter account if you don't already have one. If you're a business owner, set up a Twitter account for your business using your business name. If you're a representative of the company, set up a personal account and in your profile note that you are tweeting for your company. If you're authorized to tweet on your company's Twitter page, put your name in your profile.

If you don't have a Facebook page for your business, I also recommend that you create one. Note that this is different than a personal page: see Chapter 11.

Both Twitter and Facebook can be used to connect with current or potential customers. Use these platforms to gather feedback on new products or services, ask customers or potential customers what they want to see, or how you can serve them. Give them special "Twitter only" deals, and run contests. Chapter 10 goes more into depth about how to market your business with Twitter.

WHAT YOU SHOULD WRITE TO YOUR CLIENTS

There are five different types of messages that you can use to engage with your customers through social media marketing.

1. **Personal:** Talk about your insights or what you're doing; write out a thought, or something personal so that people can get to know you. Note: Firstly, this isn't where you can air your dirty laundry. While being personal is important, be careful to filter your messages. Information you put out on the Internet is out there forever, even if you delete it. Secondly, you could be found liable for damages if you spread defamatory information about persons or companies. User beware!

2. **Informational:** Share blog posts, photos, links, etc., of information that your customers will find valuable. It's perfectly okay to share your blog posts. Just make sure that's not all you do.

3. **Humorous:** Humor is always a great way to engage people, so have some fun! Share the little things that make you laugh during the day such as videos, photos or jokes. Studies have shown that laughter is good for the heart, so give your customers a dose of healthful laughter; they'll associate that

happy feeling with your business in the future.

4. **Conversational:** Reply to messages and conversations that other people are having. Because social media is an open network, anyone can join in on the conversation.

   Social media is a big party that anyone can attend. Conversational posts are where you'll find the most value because this is where you will be able to get in front of hundreds, if not thousands, of potentially new customers, referral partners and influencers.

   Read what other people are saying on social media and comment or reply. It's not considered rude to comment on what other people are saying because it's an open conversation. When you comment or reply you're putting yourself into the picture. Suddenly you've brought you and your company to the attention of whomever you're replying to!

   This is where I've reaped the most results: by getting involved, I've created visibility and credibility. The results have been amazing and have included my being asked to speak for national events, and being interviewed for national publications. I've even gotten business referrals! Get involved.

5. **Consistent:** You've heard the adage "Out of site, out of mind?" The same is true with social media marketing. You need to be consistently in the eye of your followers to be able to have the best results. Just like most people wouldn't marry someone after the first date, neither do results come from social media just after the first try. You've got to develop re-

lationships by staying part of the conversation over time.

MORE EXAMPLES OF THINGS YOU CAN DO ON SOCIAL MEDIA

1. Share key take-aways from a conference or event you're attending

2. Write out your favorite quotes

3. Link to interesting articles

4. Embed videos from YouTube or Vimeo

5. Ask the community for feedback on a project you're working on

6. Announce workshops or events you're speaking at or sponsoring

7. Give away a freebie

8. Have a trivia contest

9. Build relationships with industry insiders

10. Reply to movers and shakers

11. Retweet information from movers and shakers, or other people in your social media community

12. Share local events

13. Highlight the good things that are going on in your life and your business

14. Talk about recent media appearances

15. Organize a social event and invite people

16. Ask for referrals to businesses that you need

17. Ask for introductions to people at certain companies

18. Start a discussion

19. Answer people's questions

20. Share helpful hints

21. Tell a (clean!) joke

22. Give your thoughts on current events

STEP 4: KEEP AN EYE ON THINGS

Monitoring is key. In Appendix B at the end of this book, you'll find some of the best resources to help you keep an eye on things like website traffic, your social media followers, the number of retweets (a retweet is basically the same as a "forward" is in an e-mail. If some-one retweets what you said, it means that they found it valuable) on a Twitter message you've sent, the number of times your messages get forwarded, conversations about you or your business, new connections, new prospects, new customers and so on. Use these to monitor what people are saying about your company or to your company. Use them to monitor your competitors and what people are saying about them and buying from them. Check out the sites, and see what you can discover about your business's web presence.

And these aren't even *all* of the social media monitoring sites available. But they are a great place to start, so spend some time researching. Seriously, I want you to put this book down, go to the nearest computer (if it's not yours, ask before you start pounding away on the keyboard), and visit some of the sites I've listed in Appendix B. Type in the name of your business, your website address (if you have one), any social networks you've previously started or even your own name, and keep track of the results that you see. In fact, why not print them out? Later, when you're a social marketing guru, you can look back and see just how far you've come!

STEP 5: YOU'VE GOT THE DATA, NOW HERE'S WHAT YOU DO WITH IT

Hopefully you've taken some time to review your business's results at the monitoring websites in Appendix B. Based on the data provided by those sites, you should be able to see what's working and what's not.

Now it's time for you to adjust your efforts accordingly. If you noticed that a particular blog post gets a lot of traffic, then write more like it. Monitoring helps you see where you are on or off the track.

THE KEYS TO SOCIAL MARKETING

Social media marketing doesn't have to be difficult and it doesn't have to take a lot of time. The keys are to be consistent, keep in mind what's in it for your customer and give them what they value.

CHAPTER 10

How to Use Twitter Effectively

I'm addicted to Twitter! Twitter is a free social messaging application that people use to stay connected in real time, sending short messages of up to 140 characters. A social media phenomenon, Twitter has over 105 million (and growing) users from all over the world.[1] It's become a platform for meeting new people, acquiring information and getting known in a favorable way.

Let's look at some generally understood (but unwritten) rules about the right way to use Twitter. In a nutshell, they are:

1. **Don't post your personal issues.** Use Twitter as a platform where you can meet new people, gain valuable information and become favorably known. Don't use it as a sounding board for your vents.

2. **"Tweet" interesting and valuable information**, sprinkling in only a bit of personal stuff so people can get to know you. Note: Everything posted on Twitter is public record

and available online *forever*. Don't post anything that you wouldn't want your employer, mother or significant other to read.

3. **As with** other social media vehicles, **don't blatantly use Twitter to sell**–unless you've indicated up front that selling is what you're there for. Otherwise, it's the fastest way to lose followers. Instead, use it to point people to valuable information on your blog or website.

What I find to be the biggest benefit of Twitter is that it puts me in contact with people I never would have met through traditional channels. By allowing me to "follow" people who share similar interests with me (such as marketing), or who live in the same geographic location (such as Arizona), Twitter has exposed me to thousands of potential new customers!

When I post a short message on Twitter such as "I just finished writing an article called 'What is Twitter?' Check it out here!" and then add the link, I've introduced myself and my website to hundreds of new people.

Twitter is also a great way to keep up with the scoop, e.g., what people are talking about in the world, the nation, even your city.

THE FIRST STEP IN USING TWITTER EFFECTIVELY IS TO HAVE AN "INTENTIONAL FOLLOWING STRATEGY"

Simply stated, follow your ideal clients on Twitter because that is the best way to encourage them to follow you.

For example, Urban Kidz is a high-end children's retail clothing boutique located in Scottsdale, Arizona, whose ideal clients are moms with household incomes greater than $100,000 per year. With that in mind, Urban Kidz follows celebrity moms, media moms and moms who live in the Scottsdale, Arizona area. Because these women are interested in high-end and unique children's clothing, many of them follow Urban Kidz in return.

Urban Kidz also follows the media because the media loves Twitter. Lastly, Urban Kidz follows other businesses owned by moms because it wants to create cross marketing relationships with these businesses.

This Twitter strategy has been very profitable for Urban Kidz. Just how profitable? It has increased the company's following on Twitter and Facebook, and has gained Urban Kidz new customers. In fact, Urban Kidz has seen its sales increase by seven percent, even during a tough economic year!

So How Do You Find People Worth Following on Twitter?

There are many ways to find people to follow on Twitter, and one of my favorites is a tool called Twellow (http://www.twellow.com). You'll need to register with your Twitter account once you've got one, and once registered you can search for people to follow using a variety of methods.

Start searching via the "Twellowhood." You can zoom in on a map of your country then locate your area and the number of Twitter followers in a given location. Here you'll be able to see people's character bios as listed on Twitter. Once you find people who fit your ideal client mold, simply click "follow" and follow them from there.

Another way to find followers in Twellow is by searching the "Categories." You can search Twitter users by categories such as "moms," or "small business owners" or even "baby boomers."

You can even narrow down your search by using the search field and entering a query such as "moms and Arizona." I also suggest using alternative forms of the same query such as "moms and AZ."

There are many other ways to find people to follow such as those listed in Appendix A of this book.

The unwritten rule of etiquette on Twitter is that if people follow you, you should follow them back. Of course, that's not always true. Celebrities follow few people, if any. But generally, if you are on Twitter to add value and build relationships, people will appreciate this, and they'll follow you back.

IS THERE A LIMIT TO THE NUMBER OF PEOPLE YOU CAN FOLLOW?

Twitter will let you follow up to 2,000 people when you first start. From there, it requires that your numbers of followers and followees remain in a certain ratio to one another: once you reach 2,000 people, for example, Twitter only allows you to follow 10 percent more people than are following you. After that, you'll get a message telling you that you are not allowed to follow more people until you increase your number of followers.

Okay …So Now You're Following 2,000 People. How the Heck Do You Keep Track of Them All?

In my opinion, even 2,000 followers is pretty difficult to manage. That's where popular third-party Twitter applications like Tweet Deck (http://www.tweetdeck.com), HooteSuite (http://www.hootesuite.com) and Seesmic (http://seesmic.com) come in because they allow you to group your followers into favorites.

Twitter lists are a newer function on Twitter that also allow you to manage your followers. Twitter lists make it easy to see the conversations of a certain list of followers that you've created, like "media." Right now, one point of contention is that Twitter doesn't allow you to address a tweet to only the members of a certain list you've created. Hopefully that will change in the future.

There are many other free tools to help you manage your Twitter followers once you have them. Go to the "Manage Twitter" section in Appendix A to find some of my favorites.

Starting off with 2,000 followers is a great way to go. After that, let your list grow organically. It's better to have *quality* followers rather than a high *quantity* of them.

Put Twitter on Cruise Control

There are plenty of applications that allow you to automate Twitter, and I use several. But let me warn you: the purpose of automation is to maintain consistent messages while freeing up your time to interact. If all you do is send out automated messages, you might as well be spamming and you'll lose any benefits of using social media.

So what types of messages is it safe to automate? I use automation for things like weekly marketing tips or interesting quotes. Then I go in and actively engage almost daily.

A restaurant could automate its specials. Realtors could use it to automate their latest listings.

The automated tweets allow me to maintain consistency by tweeting information that is valuable, such as marketing tips or quotes. This frees me up to tweet about real time events, or whatever else is on my mind.

There are also some great tools that will post your messages to many social networks at once. Again, use these to free up your time to interact. Don't automate all of your social media messages.

 See the "Automate Twitter" section in Appendix A for some resources that will help you automate your Twitter account.

TAKE YOUR BUSINESS TO THE NEXT LEVEL WITH THE FABULOUS TWITTER TOOLS AVAILABLE FREE ON THE WEB!

This is not meant to be a comprehensive guide about how to use Twitter. For that, I recommend *Twitter Power 2.0* by my colleague Joel Comm, or *Twitter Marketing for Dummies* by Kyle Lacy.

That being said, in all of Appendix A (which you've hopefully taken a moment to peruse by now) you'll find plenty of tools to enhance and simplify your Twitter marketing strategy. I've even broken them down nicely by category for your browsing enjoyment. Go check 'em out!

FOOTNOTES:

1. Bosker, Bianca. "Twitter User Statistics Revealed." *The Huffington Post*. 30 April 2010. Web. 5 May 2010. http://www.huffingtonpost.com/2010/04/14/twitter-user-statistics-r_n_537992.html

CHAPTER 11

HOW TO USE FACEBOOK EFFECTIVELY

Do you use Facebook? If not, you're in the minority because over 400 million people all over the world do.[1] It's so popular that in March 2010, Facebook overtook Google as the most visited website on the Internet. Yikes!

What does this mean for you? The popularity of Facebook has huge ramifications for your business because it opens the doors for you to have even greater visibility on the Internet.

A LITTLE FACEBOOK HISTORY

Facebook (or "Facemash" as it was originally called) was founded in February 2004 by a few Harvard college undergrads in their dorm room as a way for Harvard University students to connect online. The platform was almost an instant hit, reaching nearly one million active users by December 2004.

Since then, Facebook has grown exponentially, boasting over 400 million active users all over the world, with more than 100 million active users in the United States alone.[1]

LET'S TALK DEMOGRAPHICS

Bet you used to think that most Facebook users are teens and college students with too much time on their hands. But as the statistics showed us in Chapter 8, Facebook demographics tell a story of incredible potential for your business.

You've got to admit it: Facebook has huge potential for reaching your ideal customers. In fact, many business owners are already using it and seeing amazing results!

SO WHY AREN'T MORE BUSINESSES USING FACEBOOK TO SAVE MONEY ON MARKETING?

Facebook Marketing Expert Mari Smith, author of *Facebook Marketing: An Hour a Day,* wrote on her blog, WhyFacebook.com:

"The Social Media Marketing Industry Report, found that **81 percent of all marketers who use social media said it generates more exposure for their business**; 62 percent said it helped close more business deals; and 85 percent of small-business owners said they reaped benefits from social media techniques.

But a July 2009 study by eMarketer revealed that though 81 percent of executives feel social media marketing enhances brands and business relationships, 51 percent of them aren't using it for one simple reason: **They don't know how**."

Start a Facebook Page

Your business should definitely take advantage of this fabulous, free opportunity.

You're going to need to set up a personal Facebook account if you don't already have one. Go to http://www.facebook.com, and complete the nice, short signup form. Don't have a lot of time? Don't worry: you can do it in about a minute, and then, voila!, you've got yourself a Facebook profile!

From there, you can add a photo of yourself and just fill in a bit of personal information. Need Facebook friends? Start with your family, friends and even business clients. You can post messages like those we discussed in Chapter 9.

Once you feel comfortable with your personal page, start a Facebook fan page for your business. Just give it your company name and use your logo as the photo. Let your Facebook friends know about your new fan page. Many of them will be happy to become fans of your new business page.

Mashable (http://www.mashable.com) recently announced that Facebook results will be integrated into real time search results on Google. This means that having a Facebook fan page can become a huge opportunity for business owners to increase visibility and get found by new customers.

7 Great Tips for Marketing Your Business Using a Facebook Fan Page

Below I've compiled a list of seven tips on how to market your business using your Facebook fan page.

1. **Give people an incentive to become a fan on Facebook.**

   Offer a special Facebook-only reward to new fans. This could be a gift certificate, discount or a special freebie offer on your web page. An e-book, report, article, video or podcast make great free offers! You don't need to incur a large expense to give something away. For my fan page, I'm putting together a three- or four-page report on "How to Tap into the Power of Facebook to Market Your Business."

2. **Instead of using a business card, give out an invitation card to your business's Facebook fan page.**

   Make sure the invitation card showcases your incentive. These cards can be created inexpensively. My graphic designer charges $150 for the design of a two-sided, four-color card. The cards can be printed for less than $50 at UPrinting (http://www.uprinting.com).

3. **A picture is worth a thousand words. Post pictures weekly.**

   You can post before and after shots, or photos of any of the following: the "best" of what you do; happy fans; your work; your store; your products; you at work; your staff; or even your events. You get the picture: pictures engage your fans.

4. Add video.

Take the photo idea one step further. Make your video less than three minutes and jam pack it full of valuable info. You can post a "How To" video, or even just a video highlighting a moment in your day. Don't worry about how you look or having the video professionally created; just make it interesting!

5. Post exclusive or "sneak preview" content.

Let your fans know that they will "see it on Facebook first." For example, for this book, I'm offering my Facebook fans one chapter as a sneak preview of what's to come.

6. Use Facebook ads to get the word out.

You can use a Facebook ad to promote your "Become a fan on Facebook" incentive. The cool things about Facebook ads are that they can be targeted to exactly the type of people you want to reach and the ads are very inexpensive. You can set a budget of just $2 a day. I've used Facebook ads and have increased my fan page membership by 50 percent using my free e-book as an incentive.

7. Build a custom Facebook landing page welcoming your Facebook fans.

This can really solidify your Facebook fan page. You could showcase your Facebook fan reward or even have a special welcome message. Here are links to some excellent examples of Facebook fan pages for businesses:

Ritz Crackers:

http://www.facebook.com/ritzcrackers?v=app_2142066
01560&ref=sgm#!/ritzcrackers?v=app_10442206389&r
ef=sgm

Southwest Airlines:

http://www.facebook.com/Southwest?v=app_19353550
7622&ref=sgm

So how do you build a custom Facebook landing page for your business? Find a programmer who knows FBML, which is the programming code for Facebook. You can find them and receive free quotes from qualified vendors on Elance (http://www.elance.com).

Footnotes:

1. Facebook. "Press Room." *Facebook*. Web. 5 May 2010. http://www.facebook.com/press/info.php?statistics

2. Corbett, Peter. "Facebook Demographics and Statistics Report 2010 – 145% Growth in 1 Year." *iStrategyLabs*. 4 January 2010. Web. 5 May 2010. http://www.istrategylabs.com/2010/01/facebook-demographics-and-statistics-report-2010-145-growth-in-1-year/

3. Smith, Justin. "Latest Data on US Facebook Age and Gender Demographics." *Inside Facebook*. 18 September 2008. Web. 5 May 2010. http://www.insidefacebook.com/2008/09/18/latest-data-on-us-facebook-age-and-gender-demographics/

4. Anand. "Income Levels of MySpace and Facebook Users." *Tech Crunchies*. 3 December 2008. Web. 5 May 2010. http://gorumors.com/crunchies/income-levels-of-myspace-and-facebook-users/

CHAPTER 12

Your Website, the Doorway to Success

Why You Need a Web Presence

These days, if you don't have a web presence, your business might as well not exist.

In fact, I performed an independent survey in spring of 2009, and it indicated that **70 percent of buyers turn to the Internet to research a product or service before they buy**. And some studies suggest that figure is as high as 90 percent! Yet it's been shown that as many as 44 percent of small business owners still don't have a presence on the Internet.[1] What gives?

Google is the most popular Internet search engine in the world. It's used so much that Merriam Webster Collegiate Dictionary added the verb "Google" to its pages in 2006. If you Google yourself and your company name but you can't find them, guess what? That means your ideal customers can't find you either.

You don't have to spend thousands of dollars on a website designer to get found on the Internet. You don't even need to be a web design genius to do it yourself. However, having a website that looks like it was put together by a first-grader can do more damage to the credibility of your business than not having one at all. After all, you only get one chance to make a first impression.

So let's get started.

ACTION STEPS:

Google your business name (just go to http://www.google.com, type your business name in the box, then hit "Enter" on your keyboard). Write down the first result.

_____

_____

_____

Google your business category and location, i.e., "hamburgers in Boston." Again, write down the first result.

_____

_____

_____

If you have a website, how far down the list does it appear? (If it's not on the first few pages, just write down the page number where you see your site.)

_____

_____

_____

Which websites do you visit frequently to get information?

_____

_____

_____

What do you like and dislike about those websites?

_____

_____

_____

List three websites belonging to your competitors:

_____

_____

_____

What do you like/dislike about their websites?

_____

_____

_____

Footnotes:

1. WebVisible. "'Great Divide' Separates Small Biz, Online Consumers." *Marketing Charts.* 21 January 2009. Web. 5 May 2010. http://www.marketingcharts.com/interactive/%E2%80%98great-divide%E2%80%99-separates-small-biz-online-consumers-7612/

"A blog is a personal diary. A daily pulpit. A collaborative space. A political soapbox. A breaking-news outlet. A collection of links. Your own private thoughts. Memos to the world."

From Blogger.com

CHAPTER 13

BLOGS: FROM YELLOW PAGES ADS TO DIARIES

We've just looked at your web presence (or lack thereof). Now let's talk about how you can spice things up with a blog. You can start one with or without a website.

YOUR WEBSITE IS LIKE YOUR YELLOW PAGES AD, BUT YOUR BLOG IS LIKE YOUR PERSONAL DIARY

Now which would you rather read? Somebody's ad in the Yellow Pages, with canned, controlled content, or a diary with some of their (possibly juicy) personal thoughts?

A blog (short for "web log"), is really nothing more than a website with dynamic content that's controlled by you. Compare this to a traditional website, which is similar to a Yellow Pages ad–that is, once it's up, it rarely changes. Some companies use the same Yellow Pages advertisement for years without ever making a change. Boring!

Small businesses should have a blog in addition to their website or even in place of a website (as long as it still provides all the relevant information). But I should preface by saying that a blog isn't for everybody (I'll get to that a little later).

Why Do You Need a Blog?

This is why: your blog is a platform for potential clients to get to know you in an easy and risk-free way. It's the "free trial offer" that will help them to decide whether or not to do business with you. Furthermore, 89 percent of journalists and other media professionals now use blogs for story research, according to a study by The George Washington University.[1]

A blog can help people to both find and hire your business. I started my blog in April 2009, and since then I've been told many times by clients and people who have hired me to speak at their organization that *"I hired you because I liked what you said in your blog."*

My blog helped them to understand *how* I could help them, *what* info I could teach them, what *value* I added to their lives and if I was *worth* the investment.

A well-written, timely, interesting and info-packed blog builds your credibility, brands you as an expert and makes you valuable. It can turn your business from a commodity into a category of one.

BLOGS ARE REPLACING TRADITIONAL WEB PAGES

These days, blogs are replacing traditional static web pages as the medium of choice for businesses on the Internet for two reasons:

1. **Blogs are very search-engine friendly.**

   Having dynamic content (i.e., content that changes regularly) in a blog format is more search-engine friendly than a static website because search engines crawl web pages on a regular basis looking for new and relevant information. If you regularly post articles on your blog using terminology that you think your ideal clients will use when they conduct Google searches, you'll boost your website rankings and make it easier for potential new customers to find you.

2. **Blogs answer important prospect questions, therefore breaking down the barriers to sales.**

   According to HubSpot Inbound Marketing, customers go to the Internet to find out valuable information about a company's service offerings, pricings, requirements, benefits, etc., so that they can make a buying decision.[2]

WHO USES BLOGS?

Blogs are immensely popular. It's no secret that credible news organizations like CNN regularly read blogs to find experts and news stories. Incidentally, many people have become best-selling authors after their blogs were discovered by publishers. In fact, recently, I was called for an interview with the *Wall Street Journal*, after the journalist had read information that I had posted on my blog!

Examples of Highly Successful Blogs

Below are some of my favorite blogs, and also some of the most popular blogs on the Internet. Check them out and get a feel for what makes a *good* blog. Make a short list of things you see that inspire you, things that you can eventually put to use in your own blog.

The Pioneer Woman

http://www.thepioneerwoman.com:

Ree Drummond started her blog as an outlet for her creativity and thoughts in 2006. She's an Oklahoma farm wife with a passion for her family, photography and good old-fashioned home cooking. She writes with candor and humor, and her blog is full of beautiful photos of her life and adventures. Her blog led to her recently published *New York Times* best-selling cookbook, *The Pioneer Woman Cooks.*

Mashable

http://www.mashable.com:

Mashable is the ultimate online resource for all things social media. If you need to know how to use Twitter, Facebook or any other social media platform, this is the place to go.

Mental_Floss Blog

http://www.mentalfloss.com:

I love to check this blog on a weekly basis for everything that is unusual and interesting! The tagline is "Where Knowledge Junkies Get Their Fix!" From Mental_Floss, I've learned things like *why cell phones are banned on airplanes*, and *seven movie stars who really were heroes.*

Now That You're Convinced, How Do You Get Started?

Blogs are easy to set up: you can even set one up for free (or at a very low cost) on many of the blog platforms available on the Internet. Take a look at Appendix C, where you'll see the annotated list of free blog platforms that I recommend.

What If You're the Type of Person Who Doesn't Want to Bother Keeping Your Blog Up to Date?

Like I said earlier, blogging isn't for everybody. To make your blog successful you need to be committed to updating it regularly. A blog that hasn't been updated for several months or longer communicates to your customers that you're no longer in business or that you've started something you can't finish (*not* a good idea for clients to have about you!).

The design side of a blog also needs to be maintained on a regular basis. For example, the widgets or plug-ins that you've installed on your blog regularly get updated by their programmers. They'll notify you about the updates within your blogging platform and you'll need to update your site. Usually this is as easy as clicking the "submit" button–not a big deal.

But if you know that you'll never touch your blog, there are other options available. In fact, you don't have to maintain or even write your blog yourself. Why not outsource your blogging to one of your employees? You can hire a firm like 23 Kazoos, or find an intern or a freelancer to do it for a nominal cost. You might even consider bribing your teenager to keep your blogging up to date!

So You're No Shakespeare

Don't let that hold you back! You don't have to be a writer to have a blog. You can post short video updates and photo updates as well. In fact, videos and photos are very search-engine friendly, and make your blog much more appealing to readers.

The Biggest Key Is That Your Blog Needs to Be Kept Current

A current blog will bring more traffic to your website and more customers to your door.

Action Steps:

What are some questions that your customers have asked you that you could easily write a blog post about?

_____

_____

_____

Who will manage your blog and write the posts?

_____

_____

_____

Which blogging platform will you use? Set a goal start date, and stick to it.

_____

_____

_____

FOOTNOTES:

1. Loechner, Jack. "Where Do Stories Come From?" *Media Post*. 15 February 2010. Web. 5 May 2010. http://www.mediapost.com/publications/?fa=Articles.showArticle&art_aid=122499

2. Burnes, Rick. "Inbound Marketing and the Next Phase of Marketing on the Web." 18 November 2008. Web. 5 May 2010. http://blog.hubspot.com/blog/tabid/6307/bid/4416/inbound-marketing-the-next-phase-of-marketing-on-the-web.aspx

CHAPTER 14

Get Listed and Get Results!

Once you get your website and/or blog up and running, then you've got to get it out there where people are looking for it. Just because you have a home on the web doesn't mean it will automatically be found.

Search Engine Optimization is Key

If you use a website designer to create your site or blog, don't assume that they've already provided this service for you. Normally this service, called search engine optimization or SEO for short, is an extra cost for website designers. Make sure you ask about it.

Get Listed!

There are, however, many things you can do yourself to make sure that your website or business-related blog gets found by your ideal clients. And the first thing is to place it on as many free Internet directories as you can find!

Here's a hint: go to Google and perform a search for common key words in your industry or service. For example, if you own a carpet cleaning company, search for "carpet cleaning" in your city. What are the results? Are there specific directories that are ranked as number one, two and three on Google? If so, that's where you need to get listed!

There are also many free Internet telephone directories, as well as local and national business directories. The idea is to place your business everywhere your customers might be looking for you!

This strategy, known as link building, also boosts your website in search engines. Here's how:

1. Link building helps you get quality traffic from relevant sites and aids in obtaining wider search engine exposure.

2. High quality incoming links make your site appear more valuable to many search engines.

3. Link building increases visibility and credibility of your site, as long as your site is linked to quality directories.

YellowPages.com

http://www.yellowpages.com: This is the online version of the soft cover telephone directory you used to keep near your phone. Customers use YellowPages.com just like they would the printed Yellow Pages–to find goods and services they need when they need them. So if you have a business, whether you market to consumers or business owners, it needs to be listed here and in similar directories.

Generally, getting listed is as simple as filling out a form and registering your business for free. In Appendix D you'll find a few of the most widely used local business directories and blog directories on the Internet.

CREATING YOUR LISTING

When you make your listing in each directory, be sure to do the following: describe your products and services using key words; include links that will drive visitors to your website/blog, thereby helping potential clients find you on the Internet. As I said, these directories are highly search-engine friendly, so this will most definitely be worth your time.

Now go get listed!

"Don't try to drive traffic to your website, go where the traffic is."

Internet Marketing Expert, Tom Antion

CHAPTER 15

HOW TO GET 9,000 VISITORS ON YOUR WEBSITE OR BLOG IN JUST ONE DAY

The complaint I hear most often from business owners who have a website or blog is that "Nobody reads it!"

I know the frustration. After investing all that time and effort in writing a blog post, to have no one read it can be a big discouragement. And after a while, many business owners will throw up their hands in frustration and give up.

DON'T GIVE UP!

That's exactly the wrong thing to do! For a site or blog to effectively generate buzz and leads for your business, **it needs to be kept current**. I said it before and I'll say it again: a blog that hasn't been updated in six months tells people that you are way out of business, or you just don't care. So before you throw up your hands and declare blogging defeat, let's look at how we can get traffic to your site!

YOUR BLOG IS UP AND RUNNING...
NOW WHERE ARE YOUR READERS?

It's simple: as my friend and Internet marketing guru Tom Antion says, "Go where the traffic already is!" I learned this with one of my blog posts.

When the Droid mobile phone by Verizon Wireless came out, I was one of the first in line to get one. Verizon had already generated quite the buzz about their new phone and people were talking about it everywhere. I Googled the Droid to see what other people were saying about it. Then on my website, I wrote my own blog post about my experience with the phone and posted a comment on an article at *PCWorld.com* titled: *Verizon's Droid: 10 Apps to Get You Started.*

My comment was:

> *"I recently got a Droid, and here's my experience. http://23kazoos.com/what-droid-does-and-does-not."*

As you can see, in my comment I posted a link to my website, and within a day that link had generated over 9,000 visits to my site!

To get people onto my site, I went to where the traffic was already, then pointed people my way. It was that simple.

Now the million dollar question is: "How many leads did that generate?" And the answer is: "I don't know." It's doubtful that any business has been directly generated from this post. But it's *highly* probable that a lot of business was indirectly generated from this post.

Why? Because the visits and traffic generated from this post have helped to boost my site's ranking in Google, thereby helping me to get "found" by more potential clients. It's like this: the higher your site is listed when someone "Googles" certain key words associated with your business, the more likely it is that they'll click through to your site. If you're on the first page of a Google search, over one hundred percent more people will click through to your site than if your site is listed farther down.

BRING THE ACTION TO YOUR SITE

So how do you make this work for you? Research your industry and your demographic, and find out what people are buzzing about and where. Add your own opinion to your site, and go get involved in the conversations on other sites. Then point the action back to your home page!

I learned a great lesson that day and have continued to successfully use this strategy ever since.

A few tips:

1. **Comment on the sites that get the most visitors.** This will generate higher rankings for your site.

2. **Post quality comments that are relevant and add value.** Don't comment just for the sake of commenting. That won't generate any traffic and might even get you banned from the site.

3. **Comment on more than one of the sites that's frequented by your ideal clients.** More comments will generate more visits.

4. **Comment frequently.** Becoming visible in your industry will establish you as an expert and increase your credibility.

ACTION STEPS:

List five websites that your ideal clients visit frequently.

_____

_____

_____

Finish these questions as if you were your ideal customer looking for the products and services that you offer. For example, someone who designs websites might write:

• How do I get a website? or

• How do I find a website designer?

Now your turn:

How do I _____?

Where do I _____?

Now enter each question into the search box at Google. Which websites are listed first?

_____

_____

_____

Note: Another way to search is to enter some of the key words that your customers use regularly to find you.

You can do keyword research on Wordtracker (http://www. wordtracker.com), or Google AdWords (https://adwords.google. com).

When you find a website or blog that is relevant to your business, look specifically for articles or blog posts on which you are an expert and that allow comments to be posted. (Hint: look for "comments" at the end of the post.) You may have to register to be able to comment, but that's a good thing as well, because most likely you'll be able to post your business information including website address. Post your comments on the websites and articles that are most relevant to your business and make sure you use a signature that includes your website address.

_____

_____

_____

CHAPTER 16

Video Marketing: What's the Big Deal?

Ever notice that there are many of us who will remember a face but not a name? I know that I've tried many memory tricks to match names and faces to no avail. That's because I'm a visual learner. The best way for me to remember anything is to have a visual aid. And there are many people out there just like me.

So what does that mean for your business and how you market it? It turns out, it means a lot!

Why You Should Post Videos on Your Website or Blog

Almost 80 percent of Internet users in the United States watched videos for roughly five hours in December 2008, with an average duration of 3.2 minutes per video.[1]

Consider this: how many out of that roughly 80 percent of Internet users are your target audience?

And how many of that 80 percent are people like me who remember things better through visual aids? According to research, it's about 65 percent of the population![2]

What better way for you to reach those types of learners than by utilizing a three- to four-minute video upload on your site?

Posting videos also ensures that your website content is fresh, which makes those pesky (but necessary) search engines like you more.

WHERE TO UPLOAD YOUR VIDEOS ON THE INTERNET

Anyone with a camcorder can record a brief video and upload it to a video storage site such as one of the following:

- YouTube (http://www.youtube.com)

- Vimeo (http://www.vimeo.com)

- Justin.tv (http://www.justin.tv)

- Blip.tv (http://www.blip.tv)

- Viddler (http://www.viddler.com)

- Photobucket (http://www.photobucket.com)

- Ecorp.tv (http://www.ecorp.tv)

Posting the video content on your website will help you reach and engage more prospective customers.

Not Convinced Yet?

YouTube (http://www.youtube.com) is the third most-visited site on the Internet, receiving over 70 million unique visitors a month.[1] Video now appears in Google search results, providing vital "Google Juice" to help your website rankings.

It's my opinion that not having a video presence in two to five years will be like not having a website today!

And here's a quick little marketing tip: **"How To" videos are a huge hit.** Make a "How To" video demonstrating how your product or service can solve a common problem. Then, name your video "How To (insert your topic here) Video," and post it on your very own YouTube Channel.

Disclaimer: In spite of all the statistics showing how successful video is in marketing your business, some of us (like me) are still terrified or otherwise reluctant to make a video. **My video marketing tip of the day: just do it.** You need to practice anyway, so don't post the first video you make, and don't give up. Keep on trying, you'll get the hang of it. I promise!

FOOTNOTES:

1. Lipsman, Andrew. "U.S. Online Video Viewing Surges 13 Percent in Record-Setting December." *comScore*. 4 February 2009. Web. 12 May 2010. http://www.comscore.com/Press_Events/Press_Releases/2009/2/US_Online_Video_Viewing_Sets_Record/%28language%29/eng-US

2. Riklan, David. "How to Immediately Determine Which of the Top 3 Learning Styles Will Work Best for You." *SelfGrowth*. 2004. Web. 12 May 2010.

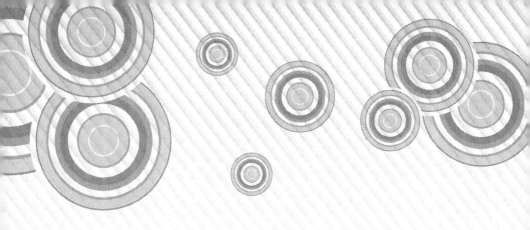

SECTION THREE

PUBLICITY

CHAPTER 17

15 Ways to Generate Successful Publicity

As a business owner since 1991, I've spent thousands of dollars in advertising, much of it for naught. I've placed numerous ads in magazines, newspapers and the like; I've sponsored a variety of events for good causes. And what have I gotten out of it? Nothing, zilch, zero... except for a huge credit card bill!

What I found is that unless advertising is done consistently, is timed right and has a compelling offer with a sense of urgency, then you're wasting your money.

GEICO's Success with Traditional Advertising

The insurance company, *GEICO*, on the other hand, provides a great example of how to do advertising right. With an advertising budget of over $300 million per year, there's no place you can go to get away from GEICO. And the company's advertising strategy must be working because GEICO has moved from the number seven to the *number three position* among auto insurers, with sales increasing every year.

We can see GEICO's message everywhere: on television, radio, billboards, newspapers and in magazines. The company's message is timely and urgent: everyone wants to save money, but especially during a recessionary economy.

However, as small business owners, most of us don't have the big bucks that GEICO has. And that's why traditional advertising is not always the best way for small business owners to go.

How Your Small Business Can Use Traditional Media

Getting your name in the newspaper or on television for very little money, however, is priceless. If you become the focus of a story in a positive way, suddenly you elevate yourself to expert status. **Having a story about your business in a newspaper, magazine or other traditional media validates your business, adds credibility and makes your business stand out from the crowd.** That's the value of publicity; it will get you noticed!

With that in mind, here are fifteen tips to help you successfully generate positive publicity for your business and get your name in the spotlight without a $300 million budget. Move over GEICO!

15 Tips for Positive Publicity

1. Make Friends with the Media:

The number one tip I can give you is to make friends with the media before you need them. Most television and newspaper websites provide contact information for reporters and producers. Many people in media also have Facebook and

Twitter accounts where you can become "friends" as well. Send them comments on stories and give positive feedback. The idea is to develop a relationship so that you can help each other out.

2. **Be a Valuable Partner to the Media:**

Once you become friends with media contacts, think of yourself as their partner. Your media contacts need good story ideas, experts and resources, so help them out! But don't just send them pitches randomly; make sure you understand their audiences, their goals and what they cover. And definitely don't spam the media; send them information that they value.

3. **Pay Attention to the Buzz:**

Pay attention to what's on the minds of the public at any given time. I recently sent an idea about "How to take great Halloween photos" to the media and got contacted immediately! If people are talking about unemployment and a recession, then your story ideas should be about how to get jobs or how to save money. The more you make your story relevant to what's going on right now, the more likely you will be to get free publicity.

4. **Make a Difference:**

The media love stories that can show heart and emotion, so think about how your business can help people feel better, and you might get featured. Recently, ABC 15 in Phoenix,

Arizona featured a story about a business that was collecting water bottles for the homeless.[1] The business's contact information was also linked on the ABC 15 web page. Talk about great publicity! So what could your company do?

5. Go Big:

This story is so big it received national attention! A neighborhood association in Portland, Maine set a goal to get into Guinness World Records by building the world's largest lobster roll during Portland, Maine's Old Port Festival in the summer of 2009.[2] The media was there to document the story and it was run nationwide.

6. Party Like a Rock Star:

Everyone loves a party! Consider holding a party of some sort in honor of your customers. Joe's Real BBQ (http://www.joesrealbbq.com) in Gilbert, Arizona, hosts an annual Customer Appreciation Event, giving away free BBQ sandwiches and drinks all day!

Joe's Real BBQ owners Joe Johnston and Tad Peelen think their annual event is well worth the time and investment. They say, "We don't spend a dime on advertising all year; this is the only thing we do."

It has worked well for them too; every year they garner thousands of dollars worth of television and newspaper coverage for days. All the publicity has helped draw thousands of people to this much-anticipated annual event.

7. Give It Away:

You don't have to do a huge client appreciation event to reap the benefits that come from giving something away, though. Phoenix area Fairytale Brownies got its start by giving away free brownies to the media and other companies like crazy. Those freebies gained Fairytale Brownies plenty of free publicity, helping it get the start that it needed to grow what is now a very successful business. The company still gives away tens of thousands of brownies every year.

8. Hold a Contest:

Everyone loves to win, and the more valuable the prize that's available, the better! Structure your contest around an upcoming holiday, such as Father's Day, or a theme such as "summer." Holding a contest gets people involved and is a fun way to spread the word about what you do.

9. E-Mail First and Use a Catchy Subject Line:

Most media professionals prefer to receive pitches via e-mail and even Twitter instead of being called on the telephone because they are so busy. A short e-mail is usually all you need to get through.

Be sure to use a catchy subject line. You've got to remember that the media are inundated daily with hundreds of e-mail messages from companies wanting media attention. You only have a few seconds to grab their attention and the best way to do that is to make your story stand out from the crowd. How do you make your story stand out in only a few seconds? With a super-catchy subject line.

10. Contact the Right Person:

Make sure you do your homework and contact the right person for the story, because if you don't, your e-mail will most certainly be deleted. Most reporters and editors don't have time to forward e-mails to the appropriate places.

11. Consider Submitting a Press Release:

In my experience, television media prefer to receive information via press releases. It's important that a press release clearly outlines the who, what, when, where and why of your story. Also, your pitch should state clearly why your story would look good on television. Remember, television is a visual medium.

Once you've written your press release, you need to submit it to the media and to press release websites. Most television stations and newspapers list their contact information right on their websites and encourage readers or viewers to submit news stories via e-mail.

12. Be Available:

It's important to be available when the producer e-mails or calls you back, because otherwise, you'll miss out. If you miss a call from the media, call them back right away.

13. Say "Thank You:"

When your story is run, contact the reporter or editor who made it public and tell them "thank you." Believe it or not, such a tiny courtesy will really make you stand out from the crowd.

14. Submit Your Press Release to Internet Websites:

Lastly, I recommend submitting your press release to free Internet press release websites. Not because they will get media attention, although sometimes that'll happen, but because it also generates traffic to your website. In Appendix E, you'll find a list of press release websites that I recommend.

15. Subscribe to Free Publicity E-Mails That Notify You of Journalist and Media Requests for Experts:

Some popular free e-mail lists include:

- HARO: http://www.helpareporter.com

- Reporter Connection: http://www.reporterconnection.com

- Pitchrate: http://www.pitchrate.com

There are plenty of great opportunities out there every day.

Footnotes:

1. Stocks, Deborah. "Valley Business Collects Bottled Water for Homeless." *ABC 15*. 23 May 2009. Web. 5 May 2010. http://www.abc15.com/content/news/southeastvalley/tempe/story/Valley-business-collects-bottled-water-for/-d1-TYWa4o6eRwMRtp32Jg.cspx

2. The Associated Press. "Huge Lobster Roll Going for Record." *My Fox Phoenix*. 25 May 2009. Web. 5 May 2010. http://www.myfoxphoenix.com/dpp/news/offbeat/dpg_offbeat_Huge_Lobster_Roll_fc_20090525_2511268

CHAPTER 18

PUT YOUR KNOWLEDGE IN A BOOK

So we've already established that the more visibility you have (*positive* visibility, that is), the more credibility you have, and therefore the more profits you have. Besides using social media, appearing everywhere on the Internet, and getting free mentions in the media, another way to get known is to share your knowledge by writing a book.

WRITE IT DOWN

It doesn't matter what industry you're in or what you sell. You have knowledge that your buyers are looking for. Writing a book establishes you as the expert and boosts your credibility.

It doesn't have to be a huge book. One of my mentors, Craig Duswalt of the marketing program, Rockstar System for Success (http://www.craigduswalt.com), instructs people on how to write a book and self-publish it in less than 30 days.

Craig teaches a daily system that's very easy and manageable. The goal according to Craig is to just get it done! One of the biggest roadblocks to someone completing their book is often the fact that they want it to be long and perfect. But Craig tells us to get over that! Your book doesn't need to be the unabridged, annotated version of *War and Peace*. It can be as simple as a 97–page, how-to guide.

David Meerman Scott (http://www.davidmeermanscott.com) started his lucrative and successful speaking and consulting career by publishing the 22-page, downloadable, free e-book *The New Rules of PR*, in 2006. The release of his book led to speaking engagements and book deals, as well as a very profitable and rewarding career as a marketing speaker, expert and consultant.

Reading David's book, *World Wide Rave*, motivated me to write my free e-book, *Build Buzz for Your Biz: 23 Creative and Inexpensive Marketing Strategies That Will Get You Noticed*. That free e-book has been a boon for me like David's was for him. It has been downloaded thousands of times all over the world, and has lead to speaking and consulting engagements worth thousands of dollars.

So don't let your need for perfection stop you from publishing. Just get your book done, and do it now.

ACTION STEPS:

Write down some topics that you could include in a book that pertains to your business.

_____

_____

_____

CHAPTER 19

Hold a Contest

Contests are a fun and inexpensive way to build buzz for your business. Everyone loves to win prizes, especially prizes that they wouldn't normally give themselves, or that are worth a lot of money. The media loves contests too, and if you do it right, your company can garner thousands of dollars in free advertising just by running a contest!

Plus, everyone who enters the contest becomes a prospect for your business! Make sure you send contestants to your website where they must submit at least a name and e-mail address to enter. In your rules, state that by entering, they are agreeing to receive e-mail communication from your company.

Keys to a Successful Contest

Here are a few guidelines to follow for running a great contest:

1. Make it easy for people to enter

2. Make it newsworthy

3. Have valuable prizes (you can enlist other business owners to go in with you)

4. Spread the word

5. Make it fun!

6. And don't forget to check the laws in your state before you get started

---

20 CONTEST IDEAS THAT WILL BUILD BUZZ FOR YOUR BUSINESS, AND HELP YOU GET NOTICED BY THE MEDIA AND NEW CUSTOMERS ALIKE!

---

1. **The "Ugliest" Contest:** This is one of my favorites and can be successful for a variety of businesses. Here's what you do: have contestants submit photos or videos of their ugliest "blank" to win your service. For example, Therma-Tru Doors (http://www.thermatru.com) sponsored a "World's Ugliest Door" contest. Just don't do something like "The Ugliest Mother" contest; it probably won't go over very well!

2. **The "Worst" Contest:** Reckless T-shirts (http://www.recklesstshirts.com), in Tempe, Arizona, sponsored the hilarious "The World's Worst Casual Friday Outfit" contest based off of the hit NBC show, "The Office." The grand prize included custom designed apparel, business cards and even lunch.

3. **Makeover Contest:** Makeovers are very popular and can be used in a variety of situations. Utah's LogoWorks (http://www.logoworks.com) sponsored a makeover contest for logos and gained tons of media exposure and new customers.

4. **Person of the Year Contest:** You can sponsor a contest for the "Person of the Year." Often times you will see this type of award sponsored by a Chamber of Commerce, but who says you can't run your own? This way, *you* get to name the criteria for winning. This sort of contest makes a person wonder who you are and gets their attention.

5. **Win a "Free" Giveaway:** Everyone loves to get free stuff, so why not sponsor a contest so they can? This is one you see all the time. For example, the NBC show "Heroes" sponsored an NBC Heroes' Nissan Mobile Device Giveaway Sweepstakes for a chance to win a car valued at over $16,000!

6. **Scholarship Contest:** Recently, an orthodontist in my area sponsored a contest for local junior high students to win a scholarship for braces. The students had to be nominated by a teacher or a counselor, and had to demonstrate economic need. The contest not only generated the doctor free publicity, but also enormous good will in the community. This, in turn, meant many new patients.

7. **"Best of" Contest:** Newspapers have been doing this for years for the simple fact that it works! What's the benefit of doing it? Because some of the "winners" buy advertising with them.

Here's how it works: the newspaper invites readers to nominate their favorite businesses in several different categories to win the "Reader's Choice, Best of Local Area" award. Then the newspaper narrows down the nominations to the top five and invites readers to vote for their favorites. The winners in each category get to tout the "Best of" award for the rest of the year.

For an example of a "Best of" contest, go to http://www.azcentral.com/best/ 2010/.

This type of contest works great if you own a publication, or are an advertising or marketing company–but just about any company can do it.

8. **"Win Your Dream" Contest:** St. Jude's Children's Hospital has sponsored a "Win Your Dream Home" contest. Your contest doesn't have to be so elaborate. Maybe it's a "Win Your Dream Night on the Town" contest instead.

9. **Naming Contest:** When one of my clients launched a new product, he couldn't figure out a good name for it. So he ran a contest to have people suggest their ideas for a great name. The winner got the product for free, and my client got a great name for it!

10. **World-Record Setting Contest:** In honor of launching a new flavor in 2004, Snapple Beverages hosted a "World's Largest Watermelon Contest."

11. **Food Eating Contest:** From hot dogs to pizza or Jell-O, you can have a lot of fun with this one! Did you know that Nathan's Famous Hot Dogs has been running its world famous contest for over 93 years?

12. **Cooking Contest:** This could be run in conjunction with a special month such as "National Hot Dog Month," or to specifically feature your brand or product. The Pillsbury Bakeoff, for example, has been a successful event for Pillsbury brand for over 40 years.

13. **The "Oldest" Contest:** Warning: this could induce some nostalgia! Host a contest for the "oldest" pair of jeans, tie, suit, outfit, etc.

14. **"Hit Television Show" Contest:** Functional Fitness, a fitness training studio in Gilbert, Arizona, launched a "Biggest Loser" contest piggybacking on the popular television show "The Biggest Loser." Pay attention to what's popular and have a contest about it.

15. **Costume Contest:** These are not only popular around Halloween, and you shouldn't limit yourself to dressing up people. Have a baby costume contest, or even a dog or cat costume contest. The more unusual it is, the better!

16. **"Design Your Own" Contest:** Threadless Tees (http://www.threadless.com) has become hugely successful by encouraging people to create their own designs and then having the public vote on the best creations.

17. **"Hottest" Contest:** Scottsdale Jean Company (http://www.scottsdalejc.com/store) in Scottsdale, Arizona, recently sponsored the "Hottest Mom" contest. The winner got to represent the company in advertising for a year. This contest, which was very controversial, garnered the company lots of mentions on television, radio and more. Exactly what it wanted!

18. **"Faces of" Contest:** Urban Kidz (http://www.urbankidz-wear.com), the children's boutique in Scottsdale, Arizona, hosts the "Faces of Urban Kidz" model search contest every year. Parents enter their children into competition to become the featured store model for the whole year. Winners receive a complete makeover, new clothes and a fashion portrait session, in addition to being featured in fashion shows, advertising and television shoots. It's a huge hit!

19. **Mystery Contest:** These contests are often popular with radio stations. They'll play the first five notes of a song and ask listeners to name the song or the artist.

20. **Scavenger Hunt Contest:** The Contra Costa Times, in Contra Costa, California, sponsored the 2009 Great Road Trip Scavenger Hunt in which it invited the public to find 20 items based on the clues that were given. According to the newspaper, the entrants loved the adventure, creativity and camaraderie. Over 400 people entered and more than 6,000 photos were submitted!

Action Steps:

What kinds of contests could you run for your prospects and customers?

_____

_____

_____

What could you offer as a prize?

_____

_____

_____

What would be the criteria for winning?

_____

_____

_____

Who would pick the winners?

_____

_____

_____

How and where could you announce the winner(s)?

_____

_____

_____

CHAPTER 20

CELEBRATE A SPECIAL HOLIDAY OR CREATE YOUR OWN

Here's a fun marketing idea: celebrate a holiday that's not well known or even create your own. For example, March is "National Frozen Foods Month." Give away free popsicles on a street corner or distribute frozen products to a women's and children's shelter. The media loves holidays because the public does, so be sure to notify the media about your special holiday! Who knows, you may get some publicity out of it.

ANYONE CAN MAKE A HOLIDAY

Creating your own holiday is super easy. All you have to do is pick a day, give your holiday a name and start celebrating it.

MAKE IT OFFICIAL

Once you've put your holiday together and celebrated it, make sure you've announced it to your clients, the media and any others who might be interested. Then you can submit the holiday to be included on the official holiday list on Chase's Calendar of Events, the definite reference guide for United States holidays and special events. There's no guarantee that your holiday will get included, but many do. My suggestion would be to make sure that the date you pick for your holiday is not overly crowded with others.

Find out more about how to submit your holiday event at Chase's website: http://www.mhprofessional.com/category/?cat=3.

ACTION STEPS:

What kind of holiday could you design?

_____

_____

_____

When would you celebrate it?

_____

_____

_____

How could you use it for publicity?

_____

_____

_____

CHAPTER 21

How to Write a Press Release That Works

Press releases are an important tool in your marketing toolbox and are actually relied on by most of the media.

Don't Worry–It's Not Too Painful

It really isn't difficult to write a press release. It simply needs to answer the questions of who, what, when, where, why and how.

Keep your press release to one page, and make it interesting. Reporters, editors and producers are bombarded by hundreds of press releases every day.

Make your topic newsworthy. Topics that are generally newsworthy to the public are new (as in, the first one ever), dangerous, unusual (as in, things that don't happen every day) or unknown. A grand opening of the area's first doggy dentist is newsworthy. A grand opening at a regular dentist is not.

Write the press release with the audience in mind. For most releases, the audience is the general public, not the media, because the general public are the ones who watch television news and read newspapers.

The media love reporting human interest stories. These are stories that show human emotion, compassion, joy, sadness and even pain.

Pay attention to what the media is currently covering. During recessionary times, people are looking for great deals, discounts and freebies, or other ways to save money. If you can submit something that will help people cut costs, that should grab some attention.

Make the subject line pop! Most media prefer to receive press releases via e-mail, so the most important part of the press release should be the subject line. A snazzy subject line makes the reader want to open the e-mail; a boring one—guess what?—makes the reader want to delete it.

Here's an example of a subject line that got publicity:

> *New Doggy "Dating Site" Means Dogs in Phoenix No Longer Have to Be Lonely!*

Here's an example of a subject line that got deleted:

> *New Dental Office Opens in Phoenix*

Condense your point into the first paragraph. The first paragraph of the press release should tell the entire story and grab the reader's attention. For example:

"Winter rains in Arizona have given way to an abundance of flowers, grasses, trees and other pollen producing plants, leaving many Arizonans wheezing, sneezing and losing sleep due to seasonal allergies. While seasonal allergies can impact the quality of sleep, men and women with unhealthy sleep patterns shouldn't automatically assume that allergies are solely to blame."

Don't forget to include the boring stuff. The remaining paragraphs should give the least important information such as time, ticket price, address, website, etc.

GET ON TELEVISION

Copied below is a sample press release I wrote for FindMyDogA-Date.com that resulted in two television segments on two different Phoenix area stations:

Title: *http://www.findmydogadate.com Helps Dog Owners to Find Compatible Companions for Their Canines!*

Subtitle: *Doggy "Dating Site" means dogs in Phoenix no longer have to be lonely!*

Tempe, AZ, July, 30, 2009- In January of 2009, Mike D'Elena found himself with a heartbreaking problem. His roommate had moved back to California, taking with him Cheyenne, his five year old dog, and close companion of Mike's dog, Mika, an American Stafford Shire Terrier.

"For weeks Mika moped around the house, depressed that her best friend and housemate were not returning. I realized that

I had few friends who owned dogs, and the ones that did have dogs lived on the other side of the valley. I needed to find someone for Mika to play with."

With that, Mike decided to find Mika a new friend. From asking neighbors, making phone calls, and posting ads on Craigslist, to what seemed like endless searching on the Internet, Mike had no luck finding anyone nearby who had a dog that could be a suitable companion for Mika.

So he decided to take things into his own hands, and three months later, FindMyDogADate.com was born.

FindMyDogADate.com is a website where dog owners can find the perfect "match" for their dog for free. Site visitors simply register their dog on FindMyDogADate.com and then search for specific criteria such as breed, size, temperament, location, activities desired and more.

All registration information is kept confidential. Registrants are able to converse via e-mail first before agreeing to meet for a "doggy date."

FindMyDogADate.com has already been an amazing success, with over 300 people who have registered their dogs since March. Phoenix area dog lovers are finding it really fulfills a need.

Of course, the biggest success has been for Mika. Every week for the past couple of months, Mike and Mika have been meeting up at a local dog park with Lauren and her dog Dakota whom they met on FindMyDogADate.com. Mika is back to being her normal, happy self again.

FindMyDogADate also hosts special events such as "Doggy Meetups" or group play dates where people can bring their dogs for some socialization and doggone good fun. The next one is scheduled for August 27th, 2009, at 7:00 PM., at Tempe Sports Complex Dog Park, 8401 S. Hardy Drive, Tempe, Arizona.

FindMyDogADate's goal is to serve as a one-stop shop for dog friendly services in the Phoenix area with listings such as dog parks, groomers, pet sitters, photographers, restaurants, veterinarians and more!

For more information or to find companions for your dog go to http://www.FindMyDogADate.com.

ACTION STEPS:

Think of at least one exciting event or announcement that has transpired for your business recently, and write a catchy press release headline for it. Once you've got the headline, piece together an attention-grabbing press release that you can submit to the online press release distribution sites in Appendix E.

_____

_____

_____

CHAPTER 22

Sponsor a Good Cause

You can create a lot of goodwill and buzz for your business by sponsoring a good cause.

For example, you can hold a food drive for the local food bank any time of the year. Everyone tends to get involved in food drives during the holidays, but food banks need food all year long. Why not do something different like a St. Patrick's Day food drive? You can reward customers for bringing in food with a small gift of appreciation–say a four-leaf clover pin or a tiny leprechaun.

Find Yourself a Cause

To find a local charity or cause, check out Charity Navigator (http://www.charitynavigator.org) or GuideStar (http://www.guidestar.org).

Below is a list of 23 great causes that your business can support.

1. Make-A-Wish Foundation

2. The American Red Cross

3. Your local food bank

4. Feed the Children

5. UNICEF

6. Muscular Dystrophy Association

7. Local children's hospitals

8. LiveStrong, The Lance Armstrong Foundation

9. Shriner's Hospitals for Children

10. The St. Jude Children's Research Hospital

11. United Cerebral Palsy Association

12. National Center for Missing and Exploited Children

13. The Breast Cancer Research Foundation

14. Boys and Girls Clubs of America

15. Local rescue missions

16. Local homeless shelters

17. Local shelters for abused women/children

18. Special Olympics

19. Local hunger organizations

20. Children's Miracle Network

21. Habitat for Humanity

22. World Vision

23. Compassion International

GET THE WORD OUT

Announce your charity cause with a press release, e-mail newsletter and social media. Spread the word and get people involved! It's just plain good business!

ACTION STEP:

What good causes could you support in your local community?

_____

_____

_____

What local organizations could use a little help?

_____

_____

_____

What could you do to help them?

_____

_____

_____

How would the publicity from your charity event help your company?

_____

_____

_____

CHAPTER 23

GIVE AWAY FREE SAMPLES

This is one of my favorite strategies by far. "Freebies" are a great way to generate buzz, create goodwill, garner free publicity and land new customers.

FREE MEANS FREE

There are certain rules you need to follow to have a successful freebie campaign, but the most important is that you must give the freebie without any expectation of getting something in return.

Recently, I saw a local television news story about a landscaping company that visited the neighborhoods it serviced and cleaned the yards of abandoned properties for free. The neighbors were thrilled. Who do you think they'll call when they need a landscaper?

To get more bang from your campaign, give your prospects a follow-up offer, such as a discount coupon to use for their first service.

THREE KEYS TO A SUCCESSFUL FREE SAMPLE CAMPAIGN

1. Give your freebie to the right people—your potential ideal customers and the ones who are most likely to tell others.

2. Make sure your freebie will have value in the eyes of the recipients.

3. Only offer a limited supply to create the need for people to act quickly.

Action Steps:

What could your business offer as a freebie?

_____

_____

_____

What sort of follow-up offer could you create to motivate people to use your service in the future?

_____

_____

_____

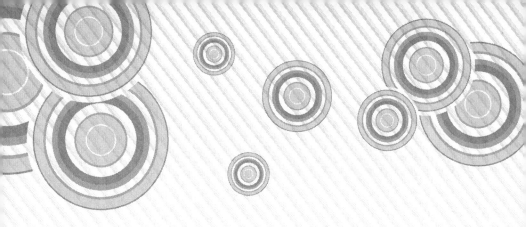

SECTION FOUR

RELATIONSHIP MARKETING

CHAPTER 24

It's Who You Know

In a society with countless businesses to choose from, a lot of the time, getting clients is about who you know.

Create a Referral Team

Team up with other business owners who work with your ideal customer in a different capacity than you. Together, you can form an alliance for sharing referrals with one another.

For example, if you own a house painting business, who might talk to your ideal customer before you would? How many people paint their houses when they're thinking of selling? Aha! A good connection would be a real estate agent or mortgage professional.

Your goal is to identify possible alliances and build mutual relationships that involve referring business back and forth to one another. By directing your clients to others who provide related products and services, you'll look like a hero.

A word of caution: just make sure your referral partners share the same values and deliver the same quality that you expect and offer! Interview potential referral partners the same way you would a potential business partner or employee. You'll want to make sure you've found the "right" person with whom to build a mutually beneficial and profitable relationship.

START A GROUP FOR YOUR IDEAL CUSTOMERS

Take the referral alliance idea one step further by starting a strategic alliance networking group.

For example, one of my ideal customers is dentists, so I formed the Dental Practice Success Center, a networking group that included a dental office construction company, dental office supply company, dental office architecture and design company, and so on. To get things rolling, this networking group met twice a month at a local restaurant over lunch. The agenda consisted of 30-second introductions, a member or guest speaker, industry updates, sharing of leads, testimonials and announcements.

Annual Fee: We originally charged an annual fee of $200 each to be part of this exclusive one-person-per-category networking community. The fees went toward creating a website and the marketing materials used to publicize the group. The only other cost that each member had to pay was the cost of their lunch!

Meetings: Our dental group met twice a month, and for best results, your group should meet just as regularly. Again, you likely can do this for no cost except the price of a meal if you meet at lunch or dinner.

Rules and Regulations: My group set strict rules regarding attendance and business ethics. I also advise that you implement a few group rules to ensure that people benefit equally.

Special Events: In addition, my group held special events just for the dentists, such as the "Dental Practice Success Power Lunch Series" to which we invited a popular guest speaker. During this event, the dentists who attended were able to earn continuing education credits.

Become an Expert: The Dental Practice Success Center has been one of my most successful marketing endeavors ever, consistently generating 30 percent of my total revenue for the last three years. As a result, I've grown to be identified as a dental practice expert by dentists in my community.

If you don't want to set up your own networking group, join one that's already meeting. There are several to choose from, including BNI (Business Networking International at http://www.bni.com), LeTip (http://www.letip.com) as well as groups that are run by business owners in your community. Check out Meetup (http://www.meetup.com) to find a networking group near you, or start your own. Contact me at WNKenney@23Kazoos.com for more information on how to set up a customized group to serve your industry.

ACTION STEPS:

What industry do you specialize in for which you could create your own networking group?

_____

_____

_____

Who else do you know that serves that same industry?

_____

_____

_____

Who would be a good referral partner?

_____

_____

_____

When and where could you have a networking meeting?

_____

_____

_____

CHAPTER 25

THE ONE MARKETING TOOL THAT EXPLODES YOUR PROFITS–GUARANTEED!

My dentist friends have a saying: "You don't have to floss your teeth regularly, only the ones *you want to keep*." The same is true for marketing your business: you don't have to be out there marketing your business, only the business you want to keep!

You've got to be out there marketing on a regular basis to keep your business healthy and strong for as long as you want to keep your business going.

Marketing doesn't have to be expensive. Often, the most effective marketing strategies are the ones that are low cost or even free.

THE MOST EFFECTIVE AND AFFORDABLE MARKETING TOOL YOU ALREADY HAVE

There is *one* marketing tool that when used on a regular basis will bring new customers in the door and explode your profits, guaranteed! The problem is that most business owners don't want to use it.

What is it? It's the *telephone*!

Okay I admit it; I'm guilty of this too! I hate to pick up the telephone to even call my mother! Is that bad or what? But the truth of it is, the telephone is the most effective and low cost marketing tool we have, because *it works!*

Here are three ways that you can use the telephone to gain customers and explode your business, regardless of what business you're in.

1. "Let's get together!"

As a former financial advisor, I was successful in one of the most difficult industries in the world for close to seven years. "Let's get together," is the one sentence that enabled me to build a successful business from scratch.

I mean let's face it, no one was clamoring to call me (or anyone, for that matter) to buy life insurance or investments. So every time I met a new person with whom I felt I'd established a rapport, I called them and invited them to lunch or coffee, just to get to know them better.

This worked well because most of my clients were business owners. I filled my calendar, made new friends, gained new clients and strategic partners, and even bought from them too!

2. "I just want to follow up."

During my last checkup, my dentist found a new cavity. When asked to set an appointment date, I said, "I don't have my calendar, so I'll call you to set one up." That was over a year ago and I still haven't called! How many people have said the same thing to you, and yet you still haven't heard from them?

If you want your appointment calendar filled up with new customers and prospects, you've got to call people and set the appointment. Because I guarantee you, they are not in a hurry to call you, even though they need you. Don't wait until they call you; call them!

3. "I just called to say 'thank you!'"

Nido Qubein, who is absolutely one of the most successful business owners in the world, has implemented a "5 a day" connection strategy. Every day he calls five of his top prospects, friends, or clients, just to say "thank you" for some way they have contributed to him or to others. Of course, he's not doing it to get a sale; he's doing it to show that he cares, and this is why it works. People want to do business with someone they know, like and trust, and what better way to help them know, like, and trust you than by giving them a call?

SET ASIDE A TIME FOR MAKING CALLS

I recommend that you set aside about 30 minutes of every business day to make phone calls. Set it up as a recurring appointment on your calendar and make it a daily habit. The more people you call, the more results you will get.

Who You Gonna Call?

There are many places that you can find people to call. I recommend that you start with your current clients. Call them just to touch base, say "thank you" or set up a lunch appointment. After you've reached out to your current clients, dig through your database and find people you've met at networking events, people with whom you've volunteered, even previous clients.

As you pick through your database, you should find endless opportunities to reach out and touch someone.

Regardless of the kind of business you're in, the telephone is the most effective marketing tool in your tool kit, and **if you use it on a regular basis, it will explode your business and bring in new profits, guaranteed**.

Action Steps:

How many phone calls do you make each day? Each week?

_____

_____

_____

Where could you find people to call?

_____

_____

_____

What time of day could you set aside to make regular phone calls?

_____

_____

_____

CHAPTER 26

How to Profit from Association Memberships

One of the first things I did when I became a small business owner was to join associations. You name it, I probably joined it.

Along the way, I learned (through trial and error) the following: the right and wrong ways to market a business through associations; which associations are the best to join; and how to make the membership meaningful and profitable.

Some Other Tips I Learned for Getting the Most Out of Memberships

1. **Don't go to the traditional networking associations.**

   I've been to many associations where it seemed like everyone was there to sell, but no one was there to buy! What I mean is, if all of the business owners are there vying for new business, how likely is it that they're going to buy from you? Pay attention to the purpose of the organization and the mindset of the people there. If everyone is throwing business cards at everyone else and talking about their business, no one is listening. An environment like this is not a good place to build any kind of relationship, let alone a profitable one.

2. Swim against the tide!

When I was a financial advisor, I belonged to the National Association of Women Business Owners. It was, and is, a fantastic organization, and I made many friends. But I struggled with turning the membership into a profitable one because there were about 30 other financial advisors as members there too, many of whom were friends with the same people I was! Frankly, I didn't want to compete with my financial advising colleagues. What I wanted was to belong to an organization where I was the "only" financial advisor, or at least, one of a few.

I thought about who my top clients were, as well as what my interests were. Then I looked into organizations that fit those criteria. What I found turned into a goldmine of opportunity!

Becoming a public speaker has been a lifelong desire of mine, so I joined the National Speakers Association as a "candidate" (aspiring professional speaker) member. I didn't join to prospect, but to learn valuable info about the industry, and to make friends.

Through my membership, I gained friends, speaking engagements and referrals, all of which resulted in profitable business. By the way, I was the only financial advisor in the organization. Many organizations have "affiliate" or vendor memberships which allow you to join without being in the particular profession that the organization represents. In fact, most of these organizations welcome your membership.

3. "I see your face everywhere!"

Once you find an association, it's not enough to just attend meetings or get listed in their directory. You've got to become involved; consider serving on a committee and helping out in any way you can. Start out by volunteering as a greeter at the monthly meeting or working on the membership committee, where you can get your face in front of everybody. You've got to be seen, and you've got to be seen often.

4. Take a friend out to lunch!

Once you become seen, you'll open the doors to building relationships. This is the fun part. Take an association member out to lunch or coffee so you can get to know each other. Do not, I repeat, DO NOT tell them about your business unless they ask you. The goal here is to get to know them.

A great conversation starter is my favorite question: "Where are you from?" Follow it by, "What brought you here?"

You've got to build relationships. This method takes time, but the kind of relationships you develop will be the ones that will last. Sometimes it may take a couple of lunches to be able to start sharing about your business, but the wait is worth it!

5. Never take your business cards with you!

Now this advice is in direct conflict with the advice of some of the "networking gurus" out there, but hear me out. I have found that when I give my business card to someone, 100 percent of the time they never follow up unless they want to sell me something. I will not do business with anyone who tries to sell me something before they get to know me. So instead, when someone asks for my business card I say, "I'm sorry; I don't have any on me today. Let me have one of yours and I'll follow up with you." Then, I put them in my database and give them a call with the goal of setting a time to meet up and get to know one another better.

6. Never sell on the first date!

Again, this advice flies in the face of the advice of some "sales gurus," but by selling on the first date, you could make a huge mistake.

I want to build a relationship with someone first; because when they buy from me, I want to be absolutely sure that my service or product is the best for them and that I can completely meet their needs and expectations. Finding all of this out takes time. I'm picky about who I do business with because I'm careful about my reputation.

7. Become a cheerleader!

I know of a mortgage professional who joined the Financial Planning Association (FPA). As far as I know, he was the only mortgage professional there in a membership of over 200 financial planners. He went over the top when it came to getting involved, making it his mission to promote the organization and its members. His tireless work on behalf of the organization helped him become the trusted resource for many of the members and helped propel his business to super success!

Action Steps:

What are some organizations that you could join to meet potential clients or referral partners?

_____

_____

_____

How would you be willing to get involved in those groups to make your face more familiar to people?

_____

_____

_____

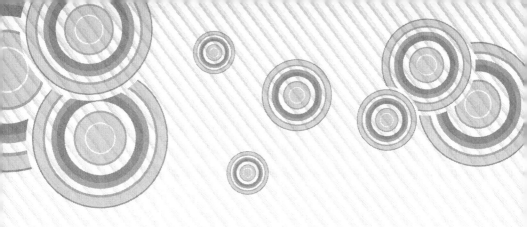

SECTION FIVE

WHERE WE'RE HEADED

CHAPTER 27

Mobile Marketing: the Future of Marketing Is Here

I can remember when the cell phone first was introduced in 1983. It was the Motorola DynaTAC 8000X, a big clunky brick of a tool with unreliable service and a cost of $4,000. Needless to say, I was not an early adopter.

I thought that it was ridiculous that people would buy a phone to talk on while they were in their car or away from their house. As with all technology, advancements gave way to smaller and more affordable cell phones, and adoption rates rose exponentially. Today, it's estimated that over 87 percent of American men, women and children own cell phones.[1] Cell phone use has become the norm, not the exception.

Today's cell phones are more useful than ever, incorporating wireless technology in a portable and neat little package. This third generation (3G) technological advancement has made cell phones more versatile than most of us could ever have imagined.

One of the most popular types of cell phones is the smartphone, an example of which is the Apple iPhone. These mobile smartphones double as miniature computers which incorporate the Internet to provide e-mail access, Internet browsing, audio and video streaming, and more. In addition, there are hundreds of thousands of smartphone applications (or "apps" for short) that put a wealth of information at people's fingertips wherever they are: need to find a local restaurant? There are apps for that. Need directions? There are apps for that as well.

WHAT SMARTPHONE TECHNOLOGY MEANS FOR YOUR BUSINESS

Small business owners need to understand that this technology is just starting out and has *enormous* potential. While it was once of the utmost importance that a small business have a website, it's now just as important for a small business to ensure that its presence is accessible via mobile technology. This could take on many forms.

Mobile Applications: Apple's iTunes currently carries over 140,000 iPhone-enabled applications, with more being developed every day.[2] Savvy business owners are using applications to keep in touch with, and provide additional value to, current clients, and to connect with new ones.

Companies like QuickBooks, Salesforce and FreshBooks have even created user-friendly mobile versions of their popular Internet-based services.

Mobile apps are quickly replacing traditional media by consumer choice. For example, one of the most popular mobile phone applications is Slacker Radio (http://www.slacker.com), a free, Internet-based radio utility enabling listeners to choose stations featuring the music they want to hear. Move over traditional ad-based radio. No wonder your ads aren't working.

If you want to reach customers in this new age of marketing, you'll have to hop on board the mobile phone revolution. Make sure your website is mobile friendly. Find the apps that feature businesses like yours and make sure yours is listed. Or better yet, create your own app. You can do so by hiring freelance programmers such as those at Elance (http://www.elance.com).

Times have changed. It used to be that people were encouraged to turn off their cell phones when going to a business conference, workshop or other meeting. Now, with the popularity of Twitter, people are actually encouraged to keep their cell phones on and tweet about the event! What used to be considered rude, is now considered good business practice!

Companies are integrating social media, via cell phone technology, into their events to interact with the audience in real time. For example, Purdue University invented a tool called Hotseat (http://www.itap.purdue.edu/tlt/hotseat) that allows students to participate in a "collaborative micro discussion" *during* class. Students can ask or answer questions, and even vote on their favorite responses. This application works in real time and operates with Twitter, Facebook and more.

Tweeting has been integrated into meetings so much so that there are PowerPoint twitter tools (see http://www.sapweb20. com/blog/powerpoint-twitter-tools) that enable meeting presenters and participants to interact live during a presentation via Twitter. Participants are given a hashtag (a unique Twitter code that designates that event) so that live tweets are integrated into the PowerPoint presentation.

Facebook also has a very popular mobile application, with over 100 million active users accessing Facebook through their mobile devices.[3] Facebook reports that these app users are twice as active on the Facebook platform than are non-mobile users.

Text messaging is another phenomenon that has become wildly popular. Have you ever been to a concert or sporting event where you were invited to play a trivia game via text, or to text your comments to a certain phone number to be scrolled across the reader board at the event? Companies like Sonic Drive-In®, Keller Williams Realty® and Subway Restaurant® use text messaging to send special messages to their customers. Check out BoomText (http://www.boomtext.com) for more information on this. And evidently, it's working. Customer testimonials on the BoomText website boast as much as 135 percent returns!

The economic recession has caused an increased interest in coupons, and according to a survey by mobile marketing firm Hipcricket (http://www.hipcricket.com), **as many as 37 percent of consumers say that they'd be interested in receiving loyalty coupons via text messaging.**

There are many companies that provide text messaging for consumer advertising and coupons. Here are just a few: Coupster (http://www.mycoupster.com), MobiQpons (http://mobiqpons.com) and Cellfire (http://www.cellfire.com).

As Small Screens Are Becoming the Norm, Savvy Business Owners Are Getting Prepared

The future of marketing is here. Now is the time to ensure that your business can thrive amidst the ever-changing technology of our world.

Action Steps:

If you could develop an application for your business, what would it do?

_____

_____

_____

Can you think of ways that your company could use Twitter to communicate more effectively (during meetings, etc.)?

_____

_____

_____

Are there any discounts or coupons that your business could offer via text messages?

_____

_____

_____

Footnotes:

1. Vasquez, Diego. "Dialing Up: Cell Phones in the Mobile Age." *Media Life*. 30 March 2010. Web. 5 May 2010. http://www.medialifemagazine.com/artman2/publish/Research_25/Dialing_up_Cell_phones_in_the_mobile_age.asp

2. Axon, Samuel. "Apple App Store Has Twice as Many Apps as Facebook." *Mashable*. Spring 2010. Web. 5 May 2010. http://mashable.com/2010/03/15/apple-app-store-flurry/

3. Facebook. "Press Room." *Facebook*. Web. 5 May 2010. http://www.facebook.com/press/info.php?statistics

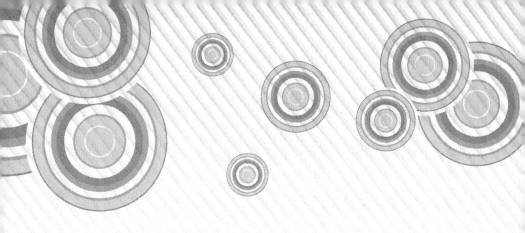

APPENDIX A

TWITTER RESOURCES

FIND FOLLOWERS & FOLLOWEES:

Twellow: http://www.twellow.com

Tweepz: http://www.tweepz.com

Nearby Tweets: http://nearbytweets.com

GeoFollow: http://geofollow.com

Streetmavens: http://usa.streetmavens.com

Twitter Grader: http://twitter.grader.com/location

Journalist Tweets: http://journalisttweets.com

Media on Twitter: http://www.mediaontwitter.com

Muck Rack: http://www.muckrack.com

Listorius: http://listorious.com

Twitter advanced search: http://search.twitter.com/advanced

MANAGE TWITTER:

Journalist Tweets: http://journalisttweets.com

Media on Twitter: http://www.mediaontwitter.com

Muck Rack: http://muckrack.com

MANAGE TWITTER ON YOUR COMPUTER:

PC:

Tweet Deck: http://tweetdeck.com

Seesmic Desktop: http://seesmic.com/seesmic_desktop

HooteSuite: http://hootsuite.com

Mac:

Nambu: http://www.nambu.com

Tweetie: http://www.atebits.com/tweetie-mac

MANAGE TWITTER ON YOUR MOBILE PHONE:

Blackberry:

OpenBeak: http://www.orangatame.com/products/openbeak

Tiny Twitter: http://www.tinytwitter.com

Android:

HootSuite: http://hootsuite.com/android

TwitDroid: http://twidroid.com

NanoTweeter: http://code.google.com/p/nanotweeter

iPhone

Twitter for iPhone: http://www.itunes.com

Echophone: http://www.echofon.com/twitter/iphone

AUTOMATE TWITTER:

CoTweet: http://cotweet.com

CoTweet enables a company to engage with customers, and monitor key words and trends. It also allows multiple users to tweet on behalf of the company.

HootSuite: http://www.hootesuite.com

Twuffer: http://www.twuffer.com

Social Oomph: http://www.socialoomph.com

Friendster: http://www.friendster.com

Ping.fm: http://ping.fm

PERSONALIZE YOUR TWITTER BACKGROUND:

TwitrBackgrounds: http://www.twitrbackgrounds.com

Twitrounds: http://twitrounds.com

TwitBacks: http://www.twitbacks.com

MARKET YOUR SMALL BIZ WITH TWITTER APPLICATIONS:

TwitHawk: Targeted marketing on Twitter:

http://www.twithawk.com

Easy Tweets: Promote your biz:

https://easytweets.com

Twitjump: Monitor your brand:

http://www.twitjump.com

Listorius: Find the top lists to follow:

http://listorious.com

OneForty: Best Twitter applications:

http://oneforty.com

Twt Apps: Applications especially for businesses:

http://twtapps.com

Just for Fun!

Twittersheep: http://twittersheep.com

Playtwivia: http://twitter.com/playtwivia

Tweetbomb: http://twitter.com/tweetbomb

Twittearth: http://twittearth.com

Twitter Grader: http://twitter.grader.com

12 Seconds.TV: http://12seconds.tv/home

Twitter Tips and How To's

100 Twitter Tips **eBook, by Dan Hollings:**

http://danhollings.posterous.com/100-twitter-tips-ebook-100-free-by-dhollings

Twitter Power 2.0, **by Joel Comm (book):**

Available for purchase on Amazon.com

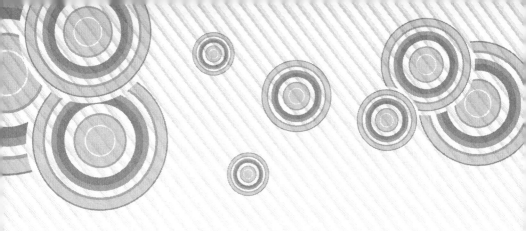

APPENDIX B

MONITORING RESOURCES

Google Alerts:

http://www.google.com/alerts

Google Alerts lets you continually see what people are saying about you or your company.

Bit.ly:

http://bit.ly

Use bit.ly to monitor the number of clicks to links you have posted. Shorten your links in bit.ly to track clicks and how your links are shared.

TweetStats:

http://tweetstats.com

Monitor your average tweets per day with TweetStats.

Site Meter:

http://www.sitemeter.com

Track your blog site traffic on Site Meter. This is a useful site for viewing the location of users and seeing how users found your site (including which key words they typed into a search engine to locate your site).

Google FeedBurner:

http://feedburner.google.com

FeedBurner tells you the number of people who subscribe to your blog.

Tweet Beep:

http://tweetbeep.com

Get free Twitter alerts sent to your e-mail with Tweet Beep.

SocialMention:

http://socialmention.com

Use SocialMention to monitor real-time social media searches and mentions. This site provides analyses including your strength, sentiment, passion and reach numbers.

Addict-o-matic:

http://addictomatic.com

Addict-o-matic monitors online mentions of your brand across search engines and information aggregators.

Twitter Grader:

http://twitter.grader.com

Use Twitter Grader to measure how influential you are on Twitter.

Twitalyzer:

http://twitalyzer.com

Twitalyzer is one of the most popular measurement applications and is used by over 400,000 people. It calculates metrics like impact, engagement and influence. It also shows who is retweeting your posts.

Company Buzz on LinkedIn:

http://www.linkedin.com/opensocialInstallation/preview?_ch_panel_id=1&_applicationId=1000

Company Buzz is a LinkedIn application that monitors who is talking about you on LinkedIn.

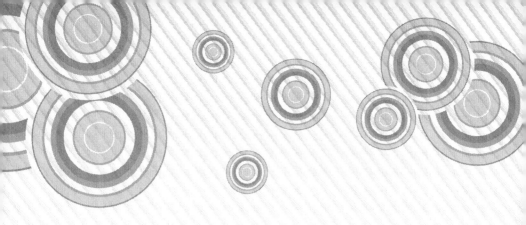

APPENDIX C

BLOGGING PLATFORMS

WordPress.com and WordPress.org:

http://www.wordpress.com and http://www.wordpress.org, respectively.

WordPress is the overwhelming choice for most business owners. It's free, simple to use, and can easily be structured to look, work and feel like a website.

I started my blog on WordPress.com then migrated it over to WordPress.org. There are major differences between the two, and I recommend WordPress.com for those just starting out.

WordPress.com is so user-friendly that you don't need any programming experience to get started. If you can e-mail, you can use WordPress.com. The cons are that your domain name will have a WordPress.com extension such as http://www.yourdomain.wordpress.com. Also, there is limited functionality within WordPress.com and limited ability to customize the site to your liking.

WordPress.org requires programming experience, but it lets you have your own domain name, such as http://www.23Kazoos.com. It also lets you use an almost unlimited number of "plug-ins" (small software "packages" that are usually free on the Internet) to increase the functionality of your website. For example, if you set your site up with WordPress.org, you can add a shopping cart, search engine optimization, e-mail signup forms and far more that you're not able to have on WordPress.com.

The downside to WordPress.org is that unless you're a programmer, you'll need to hire somebody to put together a custom design and then upload it to your domain name. I hired a freelancer to do this for me and my cost was less than $500.

Blogger:

http://www.blogger.com

Blogger is another great choice, for beginners because it's also easy to use and customizable. I like that it has many "widgets" built in for easy implementation. (A widget is a small software program that you can add to your site for additional functionality.) One advantage that Blogger has over other platforms is that it lets you use a custom design for your site (*if* you know how to put one together, that is!).

TypePad:

http://www.typepad.com

TypePad has two options: a free "micro" version and a paid "pro" version. The free version has limited functionality and no design control. The pro version allows for design and functionality control. As far as design, you can use one of their many templates or you can hire a programmer for a custom design. TypePad is a robust platform with many options for customization and it's very easy to use.

Tumblr:

http://www.tumblr.com

Tumblr is fairly new to the blogging platform world, having launched in 2006. However, it has quickly staked its claim on the blogosphere. Users like Tumblr because it's 100 percent, completely free and completely customizable. You can use your own domain name (which must be purchased elsewhere), customize your design and add almost unlimited functionality.

Posterous:

http://www.posterous.com

Posterous is another newbie but has quickly developed a following. You can post to Posterous from your e-mail and the platform automatically updates your site. Does it get any easier than that? I don't think so. There is, however, limited functionality, but the ease of use makes this site the choice for bloggers on the go.

Page.ly:

http://page.ly

Page.ly is one of the fastest and easiest ways to set up a custom WordPress site. There is no programming needed and you get your own custom domain name. While this is not a free service, about $15 a month seems to me like a small investment for a site with this much flexibility.

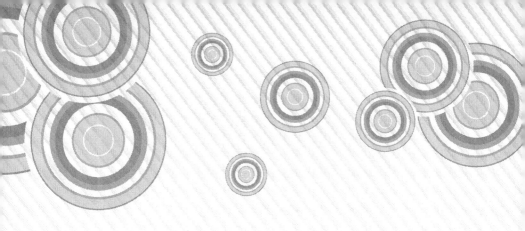

APPENDIX D

DIRECTORIES

BUSINESS AND BLOG DIRECTORIES WHERE YOU CAN LIST YOUR WEBSITE/BLOG

BUSINESS DIRECTORIES:

Yellow Pages: http://www.yellowpages.com

Kudzu: http://www.kudzu.com

Superpages: http://ww.superpages.com

Switchboard: http://w ww.switchboard.com

Google Places: http://maps.google.com/local/add/businessCenter

Bing Local: http://www.bing.com/local

Yahoo Local: http://local.yahoo.com

StartupNation: http://local.startupnation.com

Biznik: http://biznik.com

Yelp: http://w ww.yelp.com

Merchant Circle: http://www.merchantcircle.com

Best of the Web (BOTW): http://local.botw.org

Manta: http://www.manta.com

CitySearch: http://www.citysearch.com

Local: http://www.local.com

BLOG DIRECTORIES: (TO SUBMIT YOUR BLOG TO)

Alltop.com: http://www.alltop.com

Google Blogs: http://blogsearch.google.com

Technorati: http://technorati.com

Blogged: http://www.blogged.com/submit_your_blog.php

Blog Catalog: http://www.blogcatalog.com

Blog Hub: http://www.bloghub.com

BlogMarks: http://www.blogmarks.net

MyBlogLog: http://www.mybloglog.com

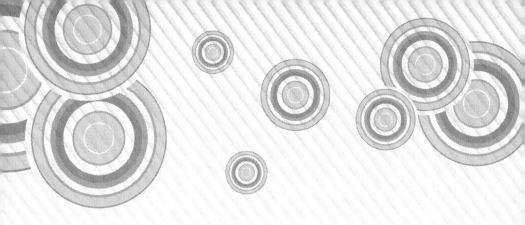

APPENDIX E

PRESS RELEASE WEBSITES

PitchEngine: http://www.pitchengine.com

Free Press Releases: http://www.freepressreleases.com

Big News.Biz: http://www.bignews.biz/blog/?page_id=9

Press Releases 001: http://www.pressrelease001.com/free-press-release-distribution-service

My PR Genie: https://www.myprgenie.com

PRLog: http://www.prlog.org

PR.com: http://www.pr.com

PRWeb: http://www.prweb.com

OnlinePRNews: http://www.onlineprnews.com

AddPR: http://www.addpr.com

1-888-Press Release: http://www.1888pressrelease.com

Media Syndicate: http://www.mediasyndicate.com

Publicity Wires: http://www.publicitywires.com

Free Press Release: http://www.free-press-release.com

Press Exposure: http://www.pressexposure.com

Press Zoom: http://presszoom.com

Open PR: http://openpr.com

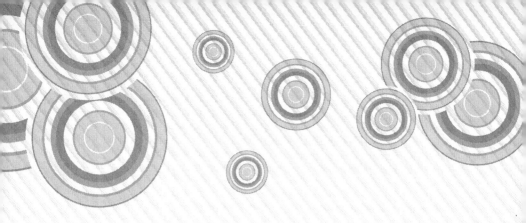

ABOUT THE AUTHOR

WENDY KENNEY

Wendy Kenney is the founder and president of 23 Kazoos, LLC, a creative marketing company that helps small business owners generate more business leads through low cost and no cost marketing strategies. She can be contacted at WNKenney@23Kazoos.com.

A popular speaker, Wendy has presented at seminars and conferences across the United States for organizations including: American Society of Women Accountants; American Business Women's Association; The Associated General Contractors of America; National Association of Home Inspectors, Inc.; Gold Canyon Bank; Women Entrepreneurs' Small Business Boot Camp; and more.

To book Wendy to speak at your next event, or to run a workshop for your company, please contact her at WNKenney@23Kazoos.com. You may also visit her website at http://23Kazoos.com

Follow Wendy on Twitter: http://www.twitter.com/wendykenney

13766245R00124

Made in the USA
Lexington, KY
18 February 2012